Califo... Public Test Prep & Study Guide 2023-2024

MOST COMPREHENSIVE AND UP-TO-DATE GUIDE WITH 6 PRACTICE TESTS!

Rick Zimmerman

&

Morris Test PC

Lost River
Publishing House

COVER DESIGN

JENNIFER LAWRENCE

FIRST EDITION

Contents

Introduction

Becoming a notary can be either a career choice or a side job to help you pay some extra bills.

No matter what reason you have for becoming a notary, you are going to need to go through several steps to become a notary. In most states, it is a process of paying fees and filling out applications.

However, there are some states where you have to take educational courses and pass an exam. In this book, we are first going to briefly look at the job of a notary and what it entails.

Then we're going to help you prepare for the notary exam by giving you some practice tests.

Part 1: General Notary Exam Prep

What is a Notary

A notary is an official who is appointed by the state government to serve the public as an impartial witness when it comes to completing a variety of official fraud-deterrent acts linked to signing important documents. The official acts are referred to as notarizations or notarial acts. Notaries are commissioned publicly as "ministerial" officials, which means they need to follow written rules without significant personal discretion.

The duty of a notary is to screen those who are signing important documents to ensure their true identity, their willingness to sign without intimidation or duress and their awareness of the transaction or document. Some notarizations will also require the notary to put the signer under oath, declaration under penalty of perjury that the information in the document is true and correct. Some documents that typically require a notary include property deeds, wills and powers of attorney.

The foundation of the notary's public trust is impartiality. A notary is duty-bound not to act in situations if they have a personal interest. The public trust that the notary's screening tasks aren't corrupted by self-interest. Impartiality also dictates that a notary won't refuse to serve someone based on race, nationality, religion, politics, sexual orientation or status.

Since the notary is an official representative of the state, they will certify the proper execution of many life-changing documents related to private citizens. Whether these documents are real estate, grant powers of attorney, establish a prenuptial agreement or perform other activities related to the functioning of civil society.

Notaries and the notarization process is responsible for deterring fraud and establishing that individuals know the document they are signing and are a willing participant in the transaction.

A notary will often ask to see a current ID with a photo, physical description and signature. This is often a driver's license or passport. This will help establish a person's identity before signing a document.

A notary in the United States is different from those in other countries. In the United States, a notary is not an attorney, judge or other high-ranking officials. The biggest confusion comes from Notario Publico in other countries, which can make it confusing for immigrants. For this reason, notaries in the United States need to be very clear about what they can and cannot do.

Those who are interested can become a notary in their home state by meeting eligibility requirements and following the necessary steps for the commissioning process. Each state has its own process, but in general, you will fill out an application and pay a state application fee. In some states, you'll also need to take a training course or pass an exam.

Before we look more at the process of becoming a notary, let's take a moment to look more at the notarization process.

What is Notarization

Notarization is a fraud-deterrent process that assures a document is authentic and trustworthy, and all parties in the transaction are aware. The notary public that performs the process uses a three-part system: vetting, certifying and record-keeping. Notarizations are often referred to as "notarial acts." The notary public is a duly appointed and impartial individual who assures that a document is authentic with a genuine signature done without duress or intimidation to ensure the terms of the document can be in full effect. The main value of notarization is the impartial screening of the signer when it comes to identity, willingness and awareness. The notary is essentially protecting the personal rights and property of people from forgers, identity thieves and others looking to exploit vulnerable individuals. Let's take a moment to consider the different notarial acts.

Acknowledgments

These are often performed on documents that control or convey ownership of valuable assets. This would include documents such as property deeds, powers of attorney and trusts. For these documents, the signer needs to appear in person and be positively identified in order to declare or acknowledge that the signature is their own and that the provisions of the document can take effect just as they are written.

Jurats

This is typically performed on evidentiary documents involved in the operation of the civil and criminal justice system. This would include documents such as affidavits, depositions and interrogatories. For these documents, a signer needs to appear in person and speak aloud an oath or affirmation of the truth of the statements in the document. The person who takes the oath or affirmation can be prosecuted for perjury if they don't remain truthful.

Certified Copies

This is done to confirm a reproduction of an original is

true, exact and complete. This would include documents like college degrees, passports and other one-and-only personal papers that can't be copy-certified by a public record office like the bureau of vital statistics. This notarization isn't an authorized notarial act in all states, and in the states where it is allowed, it can only be done with certain types of original documents.

Each state has its own laws when it comes to performing notarial acts. While different, these laws are mostly congruent with most common notarizations.

Parts of a Notarization

The first part of a notarization is the notary's screening of the signer for identity, volition and awareness.

The second part of the process is to enter the key details in the "journal of notarial acts." A chronological journal is considered the best practice, but it isn't required by law. In some states, there is a requirement for document signers to provide a signature and thumbprint in the notary's journal.

The third part is the completion of a "notarial

certificate" that states which facts are being certified by the notary. The climax is the affixation of the notary's signature and seal of office to the certificate. The seal is a universally recognized symbol and provides the document weight in legal matters since it is made genuine in view of the court of law.

Now that we know what a notary is and how the process of notarization occurs. Let's take a moment to consider why you should consider becoming a notary.

Why Become a Notary

Millions of people have chosen to become notaries, and it remains a high-demand business. While being a notary may not seem like a big deal, they hold a lot of power in the legal community. Becoming a notary is also a great way to have some side income or improve your resume. Let's consider five of the top reasons why you should consider becoming a notary.

Additional Source of Income

Although appointed by the state and serving as a

public official, notaries charge clients directly and get to keep their revenue. This is why many communities have people who serve as mobile notaries. States often regulate how much a notary charges for individual notarizations, but clients will often need more than one signature notarized. Additional fees can also be charged, such as travel, supplies and other expenses.

Notary Signing Agent Certification

If you want to become a notary to have some additional income, then you should consider becoming a notary signing agent or NSA. An NSA is a certified and trained professional that notarizes loan documents in real estate closings. NSAs are the main link between banks and borrowers in order to complete the loan. These notaries are hired by title companies directly, but their services are done as an independent contractor to ensure the loan documents are signed by the borrower, notarized and returned for processing. This line of work increases the income a person can get from notary work.

Resume and Skill Improvement

A variety of industries use the services of a notary,

including banking, finance, medical, legal, government, insurance and even technology. If you become a notary, then you'll be adding to your skill set and can improve your resume while increasing your employee value. From an employer standpoint, notaries serve two main functions: they can notarize documents for co-workers and bosses or for customers. A lot of employers value an employee with notary skills in order to handle all document authentication needs and provide additional services to customers.

Keep a Flexible Schedule

If you choose to become a notary, you can enjoy the flexibility of setting your own work schedule. A notary is a perfect job for home-based workers and those who want a job that fits their schedule. In addition, most people who need the services of a notary request them after normal business hours, so you can easily arrange a time that works best for you.

Provide a Community Resource

Notaries are known for helping people in need. If you want to give back to your community, then being a notary is a great choice. Often people need the services of a notary but can't afford the cost, such as the elderly, homeless and college students. These people often need powers of attorney, residency affidavits, advanced medical directives, college transcripts and enrollment verifications, to name a few. Notaries often set aside some time to work from community centers, retirement homes and campuses with free or low-cost notarizations. It can even be a way to market your services and network for paying clients.

If any of these situations seem appealing to you, then you should definitely look into becoming a notary. To do so, you need to be aware of the general requirements needed to become a notary. Let's take a moment to consider the general requirements of a notary before we start looking at specifics.

General Notary Requirements

Although the process for becoming a notary varies based on the state you live in, the general requirements and steps for becoming a notary are the following:

- Ensure you can meet all of the qualifications of your state.

- Complete an application and submit it to the appropriate state department.

- Pay any required state filing fee.

- If needed, start training from an approved educational vendor.

- If needed, pass a state-administered exam.

- If needed, complete a background check and fingerprinting.

- Receive a commission certificate from the state.

- If needed, get a surety bond.

- File commission paperwork and bond, if required, with the notary regulating official in your state.

- Buy necessary notary supplies.

Let's look a little closer at the process of notary training. This isn't required in all states, but several states do require notaries to complete training before they can get certified.

Notary Training

Notary training is required in the following states:

- California

- Colorado

- Florida

- Missouri

- Montana

- Nevada

- North Carolina

- Ohio

- Oregon

- Pennsylvania

Delaware requires training and continuing education for electronic notaries only.

Notary training needs to be approved by the state, so as long as you sign up for an approved course, you'll be covering the required basics during training. Although not many states require a notary to be trained, most states will support an individual's voluntary education.

If you want to undergo voluntary education, you should check with the notary regulating agency for your state. This is often the Secretary of State's office. Some community colleges will also provide educational courses. There are also a number of online organizations and vendors who will provide notary education. Most of these courses are going to provide practical information that helps you to learn how to perform your official duties.

Whether online or in the classroom, training courses will often take about three to six hours. However, optional training can fall outside of these parameters. There is also no official standard for the cost of notary training, so the cost can vary based on the provider. Online training is often going to cost less than $100, while classroom training typically costs between $100 and $200.

In addition to training, some states will also require individuals to take an exam in order to become a notary.

Notary Exam

Most states don't require a notary exam in order to get certified. The following states require a notary exam:

- California

- Colorado

- Connecticut

- Hawaii

- Louisiana

- Maine

- Montana

- Nebraska

- New York

- North Carolina

- Ohio

- Oregon

- Utah

Wyoming encourages individuals to take an at-home test but doesn't currently require it.

The notary exam takes about an hour. Some exams may require the submission of fingerprints with the state application at the end of the exam.

Another general requirement to become a notary is to have the appropriate bond and insurance.

Notary Bonds and Insurance

Most states require notaries to have a bond and insurance. In fact, thirty states and the District of Columbia require notaries to have a surety bond. The difference is the amount required by the state. The typical amount ranges from $5,000 to $10,000, but the lowest is $500, and the highest is $25,000. The surety bond helps to protect consumers. Should the notary make a mistake that damages someone, the bond will compensate the injured person up to the amount of the bond. The notary is then required to repay the bond company.

Since state laws aren't written to protect notaries but rather the public, liability insurance isn't required by notaries. This is why states require bonds instead. However, individual notaries can choose to purchase errors and omissions insurance policies since they can protect them from claims related to errors made during a notarization.

The last general requirement to consider is the notary commission. After this, we can start looking at specific state requirements.

Notary Commission

Notaries are both regulated and commissioned at the state level. This is often done through the Secretary of State's Office, but in some states, this can also be done by the county clerk or another governing body.

Depending on the requirements in your state, the process to become a notary can take seven to nine weeks. It can also take longer if the state is processing a lot of renewals. The shortest it can take is four weeks if your state has minimal requirements.

Most states have organizations that can help you with the process of becoming a notary. It can be a good idea to use one of these organizations since there are multiple steps that need to be completed in an appropriate order. In Florida, Illinois, and Texas, you are required to use specific vendors, and you can't apply yourself directly.

In most states, once you are certified, you can notarize documents throughout the state. Some states do have unique rules when it comes to jurisdiction. This can limit where you are allowed to notarize within the state or perform notarizations for citizens that don't live in the state.

You should be able to notarize for anyone with a legitimate and legal request with acceptable identification. The main restriction in some states is limiting staff notaries to business-related documents during business hours when employed by a business.

The typical term for a notary is four years, but it can vary by state. Some states can also have five and ten-year terms.

The reason for the difference in requirements is that notaries are commissioned and overseen by individual states. Since state notary laws are different, the requirements can also vary greatly. For example, in California, most notary laws are in place because of lawsuits and public damage.

Now that we have an understanding of the general requirements to become a notary let's get a little more specific. As we've already shown, most states don't require an exam. It is always a good idea to study the general rules and regulations for all notaries, as this is often the bulk of exam questions. Take a moment to consider some practice questions that can help you with the general rules and regulations for a notary.

What You Should Know

Before you take your notary exam, there are some general things you should know. While only a few states require a notary exam, fewer states actually require you to know things specific to their state. In general, most state exams are only going to ask general questions related to all notaries throughout the United States. For this reason, to help you pass your notary exam, we are going to review some key points and general notary requirements, the basic rules and exceptions, the common fines and penalties, and some key points to remember before taking your exam. Then we'll also go over some general tips to help you have the easiest time taking your notary exam.

Key Point and General Notary Requirements

- Notary commissions are valid for four years.

- Notaries can perform notarial acts anywhere within the boundaries of their state.

- Notaries need to clear a background check by having a Live Scan Fingerprinting done before they receive their commission.

- Certain actions will prevent a notary from being commissioned:

  o Failing to disclose convictions and/or arrests on the application.

  o A felony conviction within the last ten years of probation.

  o A misdemeanor conviction within the last five years of probation completion.

○ Not complying with family and child support obligations.

• Notaries are not allowed to provide legal advice about immigration or other legal matters unless they are a practicing attorney who has passed the state bar.

• Laws require a notary to perform notarizations if a proper request is made.

• Any documents that involve real property and powers of attorney require the notary to obtain a right thumbprint.

• Notarial acts and procedures include the following:

○ Acknowledgements

○ Jurats

○ Signature by Mark

○ Proof of Execution by Subscribing to Witness Certificates

○ Certified Copies of Power of Attorney

○ Certified Copies of the Notary's Journal

● In order for a document to be notarized, it needs to meet three criteria:

○ The document must be complete.

○ The document must contain the signature of the principal.

○ The document must have the correct notarial wording.

● Notarial Acts can only be completed by the notary and not the signer.

● Notarial wording can appear on the document or on a loose-leaf certificate.

● The four-step process for performing a notarization needs to be completed in entirety:

○ Identifying the signer.

○ Completing the journal entry.

○ Signing by the principal/signer and using the right

thumbprint when necessary.

  ○ Fill out the notarial act/wording.

• The notary's sequential journal and seal/stamp need to be kept under the exclusive and direct control of the notary.

Notary Rules and/or Exceptions

• Signers must be identified through Satisfactory Evidence, which is done through one of three processes:

  ○ Specific Paper Identification Documents

  ○ Oath of a Single Credible Witness

  ○ Oath of Two Credible Witnesses

• The maximum fee a notary can charge is $15, with the following exceptions:

  ○ Depositions can charge $30, with the administration of oath being $7 and the certificate to the deposition another $7. But never higher than a charge of $44.

- The signer of the document needs to personally appear before the notary in order for their signature to be notarized. With the following exceptions:

  o A subscribing witness can be used when a signer has another person prove to the notary that they signed the document.

- Signers need to sign both the document and the notary journal. With the following exceptions:

  o A signature by mark can occur when the signer is unable to sign or write their name. The signer should have the document notarized by marking a mark in the presence of two witnesses.

- A notary notarizes signatures, but they don't certify documents. With the following two exceptions:

  o Copies of the notary's own journal.

  o Copies of a Power of Attorney.

- Notaries have a 30-day rule to reply to the Secretary of State with three exceptions:

○ If their stamp/seal is lost or stolen, then an immediate reply is warranted.

○ If their journal is lost or stolen, then an immediate reply is warranted.

○ If their journal is taken by a peace officer, then a ten-day reply is warranted.

• The notary must use their stamp/seal on all notarized documents, with the exception of Subdivision Maps.

• A notaries seal/stamp can't be surrendered to anyone with the following exceptions:

○ A court/judge can require the surrender of the seal/stamp after a commission is revoked when the notary is convicted of a crime related to Notarial Misconduct, including the false completion of a notarial certificate or a felony. In this instance, two things must be noted.

■ The court/judge forwards the seal to the Secretary of State with a certified copy of the conviction judgment.

■ This is the only time someone is allowed to possess the notary seal since you need to destroy the notary seal when the commission is no longer valid.

• The journal needs to be kept under the notary's exclusive and personal control at all times. No one is allowed access to the information in the journal, with the following exceptions:

○ Members of the public can get a lined item copy of the journal with a written request.

○ Under a court order, the examination and copying of the journal can be done in the notary's presence.

○ An employer can perform a business examination and copying of the journal in the presence of the notary.

Common Fines and Penalties

• A $75,000 fine is applied in the following circumstance:

○ Deed of Trust Fraud. This is the willful fraud and false filings in connection with a Deed of Trust on a Single-Family Residence.

• $10,000 penalties occur in two situations:

○ Identity of the Credible Witness. This is the failure to obtain the satisfactory evidence needed to establish the identity of a single credible witness.

○ Penalty of Perjury/Acknowledgement. This is when someone willfully states as true a material fact and/or falsifies a certificate of acknowledgment.

• $2,500 civil penalties can be applied in two circumstances:

○ Failing to provide a notary journal to a peace office when requested.

○ Failing to obtain the required thumbprint.

• $1,500 violations are willful and intentional violations. They can be the following:

○ Using false or misleading advertising where the notary public represents that they have duties, rights or privileges that they don't possess.

○ Committing any act that involves dishonesty, fraud or notarial misconduct.

○ Executing any certificate as a notary that contains a statement known to be false to the notary.

○ Violating the prohibition against a notary who holds themselves as an immigration specialist or consultant advertising or

■ Violating the restrictions on charging to assist in completing immigration forms and

■ Violating the restrictions on advertising notarial services in a language other than English

○ Translating the words "notary public" into Spanish.

○ Failing to fully and faithfully discharge any of the duties or responsibilities required of a notary public.

○ Unauthorized manufacturing, duplicating or selling the public seal of a notary.

○ Failing to notify the Secretary of State that a public seal is lost, stolen, destroyed or damaged.

• $1,000 fine is applied in the following situation:

o Unlawful Practice of Law. This is when any person is practicing law but is not an active member of the State Bar.

• $750 violations are not willful oversights that can still be considered violations. This includes the following:

o Failing to discharge notary duties.

o Charging more than the prescribed fees stated by notary law.

o Failing to complete the acknowledgment at the time the signature and seal are affixed to the document.

o Failing to administer the oath or affirmation as required.

o Accepting improper identification.

• $500 infraction penalties apply in the following situation:

o Failing to notify the Secretary of State in two situations

■ Changing a business, mailing or residential address and

■ Changing the name of the notary public.

Along with these penalties, a denial of an application or suspension or revocation of the notary commission can occur. If a person is guilty of a misdemeanor and/or felony, they can also be liable in a civil action for damages.

Key Points to Know

• Certain notarial acts require specific wording. This includes the following:

○ For an acknowledgment, the following specifics are needed:

■ This is the most common form of notarization

■ It must be done in the notary's presence

■ The notary needs to positively identify the signer

■ The signer needs to acknowledge signing the

document

■ Out-of-state acknowledgments are allowed as long as the certification doesn't require the notary to supersede the notarial law in their practicing state

○ For a jurat, the following specifics are needed:

■ This is the second most common form of notarization.

■ The signer must sign the document in the notary's presence.

■ The notary must administer a separate oath for each jurat.

■ Out-of-state jurats aren't acceptable, and a loose-leaf jurat needs to be used.

○ For proof of execution by a subscribing witness certificate, the following specifics are needed:

■ This document is used when the document principal/signer can't personally appear before the notary.

■ This document can't be used on any documents that

affect real property or on documents that require a thumbprint in the notary's journal.

■ The subscribing witness needs to be identified by a credible witness with an acceptable form of identification.

■ There has to be an unbroken chain of personal knowledge:

• The notary needs to know the credible witness, the credible witness needs to know the subscribing witness, and the subscribing witness needs to know the principal.

• Notaries are allowed to notarize documents in any language they can't speak or read since they aren't responsible for the contents of the documents, provided the notarial wording is in English.

• Notaries can't notarize documents for a signer that they are unable to communicate. And they can't use an interpreter.

• When completing a notarization with a signature by mark, the following applies:

○ The process requires two viewing witnesses who

observe the principal/signer making their mark on the document and in the notary's journal.

○ The viewing witnesses don't have to be identified, but they do need the following:

■ They must sign the document as witnesses.

■ The witness must cursive the principal/signer's name next to the mark on the document.

■ The witness or the notary needs to write the principal/signer's name next to the mark in the notary's journal.

• The notary must take, subscribe and file the oath of office and file a surety bond with the county clerk's office or place of business as stated in the application within 30 calendar days from the date of the commission.

• Errors and Omissions Insurance can be purchased to protect a notary who damages someone as a result of notarial misconduct or negligence. This can even be true in the following situations:

○ Even simple oversights like failing to affix a notary

seal or properly identify a principal/signer can subject the notary to being personally liable for losses and/or damages.

• A notary public is allowed to notarize for relatives as long as don't so doesn't provide a direct financial or beneficial interest to the notary.

• The employer of a notary can limit notarization to the following in the ordinary course of employment:

○ Who and when to notarize and

○ How much the notary can charge for their services

• Notaries are prohibited from providing legal advice and/or practice law unless they are also a licensed and practicing attorney.

These are the general facts that apply to notaries in all states. This information forms the basics of what is covered in most notary exams in states that require them. Knowing this information is the first step in helping you pass your notary exams. The next thing you need to do is prepare for your notary exam. Even in states where the exam is a handful of open-book questions, it can be a good idea to prepare and study in advance. Let's consider some practical tips to help you study for and prepare to take the notary exam.

Preparing for the Notary Exam

   The notary public is responsible for verifying signatures on important legal and real estate documents. Most states require notaries to have some level of education before getting a commission, and a few states require individuals to take a licensing exam in order to show they understand the basic knowledge of notary laws and the role they play in society. Tests are often done at testing centers in written form or online, and the exact requirements will vary by state. You'll often have plenty of time to prepare for your exam, and the following are some tips to help you prepare for the notary exam if it is required in your state.

Study Guides and Handbooks

The licensing authority of the state in which you want to serve as a notary public will provide guidelines for taking the exam. This will often include a handbook. The handbook for the state will provide all aspects of becoming a notary public, the laws that need to be followed and the specific duties of a notary public as allowed in that state. By studying these handbooks, you can get a good idea of what specific state information may be on the exam in addition to the general guidelines and information we listed above.

Review Notary Public Laws and Recent Cases

You can also research online about notary public laws for your state. This can often be found online at the state legislature home page and a search of the words notary public. This will be the easiest way to find the most recent applicable legislation. The full texts of the laws are often available on the website of the agencies that issue licenses. For example, the Secretary of State in New York provides full texts of their laws online. You can also search for recent court cases that involve potential errors by notaries public so you can have some real-life examples of the application of notary laws.

Study Potential Scenarios

Take a moment to look up frequently asked questions and common requests for notaries. Many state agencies that license notaries will have this information on their websites. For example, California offers these questions and their associated answers online. Playing out potential scenarios is a great way to help you understand the laws and the appropriate actions you should take. This practice can help you when it comes to answering multiple-choice questions related to the decision-making process of notaries. For example, as a notary, you may be asked to notarize a document that you didn't personally view the signing of and choosing the right action in the situation can be a real question on an exam.

Test Questions and Practice Tests

The last thing you can do is consider taking practice

tests and questions. Self-testing can help you check your research and see what areas you need to increase your research. There are paid practice tests you can take online, but for a simple general question test, you can often do this on your own with a few sample questions, such as you'll get in the upcoming practice tests of this book.

All of these things are going to help you prepare for your notary exam. Now let's provide you with some practice tests to get ready for your notary exam. First, we'll provide some general notary exam practice questions and answers for you to prepare with, then we'll look at some specific examples of questions.

General Notary Exam Practice Questions

What is the term for individuals who receive services from notaries?

Constituents.

What services does a notary commonly provide?

Taking acknowledgments, administering oaths and affirmations, executing affidavits and taking depositions.

Are notarized documents admissible in court?

Yes. Documents are considered valid and establish "prima facia" evidence or presumptive evidence.

Is a notary public considered a commissioned public officer?

Yes. The notary public is appointed by the Secretary of State by Executive Law.

Why do people need a notary?

Notaries authenticate signatures, compel truthfulness from others and help to reduce the risk of fraud.

What are notaries NOT responsible for?

A notary isn't responsible for guaranteeing the accuracy or truth of any statements in the documents they are notarizing.

What notarial act is the most commonly performed?

The acknowledgment is found in deeds, mortgages and other associated real estate documents and other areas not related to real estate.

What are the potential sizes for a notary stamp?

Notary stamps should be 1 inch in width and 2 ½ inches in length.

If a regulation states up to 30 days, what does this mean?

This means calendar days.

What shape must a notary stamp be?

A notary stamp must be rectangular in shape.

What are the requirements for two credible witnesses?

There are no specific requirements.

Subscribing witnesses can come to a notary with which documents?

A homestead declaration.

A notary who willingly and knowingly notarizes a fraudulent real estate document is guilty of what?

The notary is guilty of a felony.

A new notary certificate is awarded by whom?

The Secretary of State.

What code allows notaries to certify a copy of a power of attorney?

The Probate Code.

Under the signature-by-mark process, how many people must write the name of the X signer?

At least one individual.

How long do you have to report a move to the proper authority?

You have 30 days.

When making a false statement, what is the statute of limitations?

Four years.

What isn't required on a passport?

The signature of the notary.

An ID must have what?

An ID must have a picture, a physical description and a signature.

Notaries must do what with their journal and stamp?

The journal and stamp must remain under the direct control of the notary.

Where are you to deliver your papers when you resign from a commission?

The county clerk where you have your current oath on file.

What isn't required when taking an oath?

You are not required to raise your right hand.

Notary certificates must be signed by whom?

Certificates must be signed by the notary.

An acceptable ID must be issued within what time frame?

Within the last 5 years.

After giving your journal to the proper authority, you have how long to notify the Secretary of State?

You have 10 days.

When moving, you must contact which authority?

You must contact the Secretary of State.

Who has the authority to take your journal?

A peace officer who has probable cause.

What is a notary not required to do regarding a fee?

A notary is not required to charge a fee.

Which documents require the signer to leave a right thumbprint?

A Power of Attorney and a Trust Deed for real estate.

What is an affirmation?

It is the legal equivalent to an oath but has no referral to a Supreme Being.

What is a notary not allowed to notarize?

A notary cannot notarize real estate documents when they are a mortgagor in a transaction.

A certificate of authorization can be provided by whom?

Only from the Secretary of State.

When it comes to reproductions, what does a certified copy certify?

A certified copy certifies that the reproduction is accurate.

Notaries cannot perform their actions when serving in what other capacity?

Notaries cannot perform services when they are named as a principal in a financial transaction.

What does an acknowledgment certify?

An acknowledgment certifies that a signer's identity was satisfactorily proven, the signer admits to signing the document, and the signer appeared before the notary.

Where do notaries get their seals from?

Only from approved vendors and manufacturers.

Who can bring a document to a notary if the principal is unable to appear?

A subscribing witness.

A subscribing witness is placed under oath and asked what?

The subscribing witness is asked three things: 1) Did you sign as a witness? 2) Did the signer acknowledge their signing? 3) Did the signer ask for the document to be notarized?

When is the term for when a subscribing witness brings the document?

Proof of Execution

If someone inherits property in another state and they need to send an affidavit to the court, what can a notary do?

A notary can do a notarization process.

What must be signed in the presence of a notary?

A Jurat.

If someone influences a notary to perform improperly, they are guilty of what?

They are guilty of a misdemeanor.

An oath is defined as what?

An affirmation or a solemn spoken pledge.

A notary needs to rely on what to provide satisfactory evidence of identity?

ID cards and business card photos.

The notary is obligated to do what?

A notary is required to reimburse a surety company for any bond funds that are paid out.

A notary may perform what additional services?

A notary can notarize documents in a foreign language,

and they can notarize a relative's documents.

Notaries are allowed to withhold services to whom?

A notary working for an employer can limit services to transactions related to the employer's business. A notary may also withhold services if a document is incomplete or if they believe an individual doesn't know what they are signing.

Is an embossed seal required?

An embossed seal is acceptable but not required.

Credible witnesses cannot be linked to a document in which way?

Credible witnesses can't have a financial interest in the document.

When it comes to a military notary, what are the charges?

A military notary can't charge any fees.

What is the employer of a notary allowed to do in regard to the notary journal?

The employer may copy journal entries related to the business in front of the notary.

The security bond for a notary protects whom?

The security bond protects the public.

The Venue in a document refers to which county?

The county where the signer personally appeared.

What should a notary do if they are asked to notarize an incomplete document?

A notary should refuse to notarize the document.

What is the most commonly completed form?

An acknowledgment.

What items must be recorded in a journal each time?

The date, time, type of document and fees.

A notary cannot advertise what?

A notary cannot advertise the Spanish terms *notario publico* or *notario.*

A credible identifying witness serves what main

purpose?

The credible identifying witness serves to identify the signer.

The seal must include what elements?

The seal must include three elements: 1) The state seal and the notary's name. 2) The expiration date of the commission and county where the oath is on file. 3) A sequential ID number of the manufacturer and the notary's sequential commission number.

An individual who is starting a business as an immigration consultant cannot advertise what?

They cannot advertise themselves as a notary public.

The notary seal must contain what?

The notary seal must contain three elements: 1) Be

photographically reproducible and have an expiration date. 2) Contain the state seal and the words notary public. 3) Have a serrated or milled edge border.

What must a notary do if the signer can't provide a right thumbprint?

The notary may use the left thumb or any available finger as long as a note of the problem is provided.

Which documents don't require a seal?

A seal isn't required on subdivision maps.

After a request for a transaction, the notary has how many days to respond?

Fifteen days.

Someone who poses as a notary but is not commissioned is guilty of what?

A misdemeanor.

A notary who resigns their position with an employer must do what?

The notary must notify the Secretary of State of any business address change.

Why must there be two witnesses for a signature by mark?

To view or acknowledge the making of the mark.

What must be included in a written request for a photocopy of a journal entry?

The type of document, month and year of notarization and names of the parties involved.

If a notary and private employer enter into an agreement, then what happens in regard to notary actions?

Notary actions are limited to business transactions.

What documents can't a notary certify?

A journal entry requested by a member of the public.

Proof of execution can be done on which document?

A Deed of Reconveyance.

The name on the Subscribed and Sworn line of a certificate is whose?

The name of the signer.

A notary and their employer have what right?

To limit notary services solely to their business.

A notary cannot charge a fee for which notarizations?

A circulator's affidavit.

Notaries who engage in an unauthorized practice can have their commission?

Denied, revoked or suspended.

What may the notary use their commission for?

The notary may use their commission to notarize for veterans.

If a notary uses the term notario publico in an advertisement, then their commission can be what?

Suspended for no less than one year and revoked after two offenses.

Under what circumstances can a notary not be automatically disqualified from performing a notarization?

When the notary is serving as a real estate agent.

A notary who doesn't deliver their papers to the county clerk after their commission expires is guilty of what?

A misdemeanor.

A driver's license that has been expired for 52 months is presented to a notary; what should the notary do?

The notary can use it as an acceptable form of

identification.

The right thumbprint isn't needed in the journal for which situation?

In a Deed of Reconveyance.

When notarizing documents for friends, a notary needs to make what note in their journal?

The signer's driver's license number, the type of document and the notary's fee.

Under what circumstances can a commission be suspended and/or revoked?

When a notary doesn't pay child support.

A notary can notarize for a family member when they

are acting in what role?

When the notary is acting as an employee.

When making a witness swear an oath, what phrase can be used?

The phrase "under penalty of perjury."

Should a notary public die, their personal representative must do what?

They should promptly notify the Secretary of State and send all papers and records to the county where the notary's oath is recorded.

When a signer is making a signature by mark, what must happen?

The signer must place their mark in the notary's journal.

What must be included in a journal?

The character of each document.

If the last day for filing an instrument or other document falls on a Saturday or holiday, the act should be performed; when?

By the next business day.

If the notary's certificate is previously filled with an incorrect state and county, what must the notary do?

A line must be drawn through the inappropriate words with the correct state and county then being written in the document.

What is the main purpose of an acknowledgment?

To authenticate signatures and require a personal appearance.

If a person coerces a notary to perform improperly, they are guilty of what?

A misdemeanor.

What doesn't a notary need to record in their journals?

The signer's address.

If the credible witness knows both the signer and the notary personally, then what happens?

Only one witness will be needed.

A notary public can notarize a document if they have done what?

If a document is in a foreign language.

A notary cannot charge fees when verifying what document?

A nomination document or circulator's affidavit.

What is a notary allowed to do if their employer asks to see the journal used in the business to see who is providing the most business?

The employer is allowed to only see items that pertain to the business.

A notary can notarize documents that will be filed in another state, but they can't do what?

They can't certify the signer holds a particular capacity.

If a notary works for a city, county or state agency, then fees collected for non-agency notarizations go to whom?

The notary public must remit them to the employing agency.

What must the notary do when notarizing a document containing an acknowledgment?

The notary may accept a document that has already been signed.

When should an oath be involved in an acknowledgment?

When the signer uses a credible witness as their form of ID.

The notary should accept what to establish the proper

ID of the principal?

The notary can accept one of three things: 1) Two credible witnesses with IDs who personally know the principal. 2) A credible witness who personally knows the notary and the principal with proper ID. 3) A proper ID from the principal that is current or issued within the last five years.

What additional item is needed with a foreign passport?

A stamp from a US Immigration Agency.

If a notary faces a judgment of $22,000 and their bond pays $15,000, then how much is the notary liable for?

The notary is liable for $22,000.

How is a subscribing witness identified?

By one credible witness known to the subscribing witness and the notary with an ID.

A notary seal and signature can't be affixed to a document without what?

Notarial wording.

Foreign language advertising regulations have strict rules with one exception?

A single desk plaque.

The Secretary of State will give written notice when a check isn't honored for payment. With no correction, the second notice of cancellation is effective when?

In 20 days.

If a public agency pays the employee's expenses, then what happens with the fees?

The fees are remitted to the agency.

What must a notary do if they are unable to communicate with a customer?

The notary should refer them to someone who speaks their language.

What key wording is found in an acknowledgment?

Personally appeared.

A notary needs to do what in order to meet the 30 calendar day filing limit for the oath with the county?

The notary should allow for any type of delay.

What are the exceptions to an appearance by the principal?

A subscribing witness.

What is one main purpose of a jurat?

It is to make sure the signer signs in front of the notary.

How must the notary communicate a change in address to the Secretary of State?

This can be done in one of three ways: 1) The notary must communicate the change when it is a business address. 2) The notary must communicate the change when it is a residential address. 3) The communication must be by certified mail within 30 days.

What is an attest or attestation?

The completion of a certificate by a notary who has done a notarial act.

What is a commission?

It is the empowerment to perform notarial acts and the written evidence of authority to perform said acts.

What is an acknowledgment?

It is a notarial act in which the notary certifies that three things occurred: 1) The individual appeared before the notary. 2) The individual is personally known by the notary or identified through satisfactory evidence. 3) The signature was the individual, and the signed record was done in the presence of the notary.

What is a commissioning date?

It is the date entered on the commissioning or

recommissioning certificate for a notary.

What is an appointment or appoint?

It is the process of naming an individual to the office of notary public after determining the individual has complied with all requirements.

What are the various definitions and levels of a crime?

A crime can be defined in five different levels: 1) An attempt to commit a crime. 2) An accessory to the commission of a crime. 3) Aiding and abetting a crime. 4) Conspiracy to commit a crime. 5) Solicitation to commit a crime.

What is a jurat?

A notary certificate that evidences the administration of an oath or affirmation.

What is an appointee?

It is an individual who has been appointed or reappointed to the office of notary public but hasn't yet taken the oath of office to be commissioned.

What does an acknowledgment acknowledge?

The acknowledgment provides three things: 1) The individual appeared in person and provided a record. 2) The individual was personally known to the notary. 3) The document was signed while in the physical presence of the notary or indicates that the signature is their own.

Who is an applicant?

A person who seeks an appointment or reappointment to the office of notary public.

Who is a credible witness?

An individual who is personally known to the notary and to whom two things apply: 1) The notary believes the individual is honest and reliable. 2) The notary believes the person is not a party to or a beneficiary of the transaction.

What is an affirmation?

A notarial act that is the legal equivalent to an oath in which the notary certifies that at a single time and place, the following occurred: 1) The individual appeared in person. 2) The individual was either known to the notary or provided the required identification. 3) The individual made a vow of truthfulness under penalty of perjury based on personal honor and without invoking a deity or using any form of the word "swear."

What is an attestation?

It is the completion of a certificate by a notary after

performing a notarial act.

How long must a notary retain their journal?

Ten years.

If a notary receives a document that doesn't have a notary certificate, they should do what?

The notary should ask the signer to determine the type of certificate based on the plain meaning of notarial acts.

If someone requests to view the notary journal, they may only do so under what circumstances?

It must be within the physical presence of the notary.

If a document isn't in English but has a notarial certificate in English, can a notary still notarize the document?

Yes.

When a notary's commission is revoked by the
Secretary of State, what happens?

Three things happen: 1) You are not allowed to receive
a notary commission in any state. 2) You must follow the
legal resignation rules. 3) You can be at risk for civil and
criminal liability.

If a notary is not a lawyer, they can't do what?

A notary who isn't a lawyer can't do three things: 1)
Advise a client which certificate to use on a document. 2)
Engage in any unauthorized practice of law. 3) Advertise
yourself as an expert in immigration matters.

California State Notary Exam

California is second to New York when it comes to the most difficult application requirements for notaries. In addition to an exam, the state also requires an education course and a background check. The exam itself is one of the most challenging of all states. The test is based on the Notary Public Handbook. It is a proctored exam, and individuals need to score a minimum of 70 percent in order to get commissioned by the state of California. The exam must be re-taken each time the commission is renewed. Try your hand at a couple of practice questions below.

Name one requirement to become a notary in the state of California?

You must be a legal resident of the state of California.

What is one possible penalty in California for perjury?

In California, the penalty for perjury is 2, 3 or 4 years in prison.

How long does the state of California have to respond when you file a request for a New Certificate of Authorization?

The state has 5 days to respond.

What is the policy of using the term notario publico in the state of California?

The use of the term notario publico in California is prohibited.

Are death certificates required to be notarized in the state of California?

Death certificates are not notarized in the state of California.

What is the penalty for stating a known false fact is true?

The penalty for stating a false fact is true is $10,000.

When does California officially recognize you as a notary?

The state of California recognizes a new notary once they have filed an oath and bond.

What is the fine for overcharging for a non-immigration form?

The fine can be up to $750.

Failing to provide a peace officer with your journal when requested is punishable by a civil penalty up to what amount?

A fine of up to $2,500.

As a notary, you are required to post signs in English and any other language you use that you are not an attorney and cannot provide legal advice. What is the fine for failing to do this?

A fine of up to $1,500 and at least a year suspension of your notary commission and a revocation of the commission for life on the second offense.

If you fail to notify the state that your journal or stamp is lost, what is the potential fine?

The fine can be up to $1,500.

Who cannot notarize documents in the state of California?

A trustor or trustee of a document.

After your commencement date, you have how long to take your oath of office?

You have 30 days.

What is the jurisdiction of a notary in California?

Notaries can practice within the entire state of California.

If your commission is filed on the first of the month and you file your oath on the 25th of the month, when does your commission expire?

The end of the previous month in four years.

How long is a commission valid?

A commission is valid for 4 years in the state of California.

How much is a four-year notary bond worth?

A bond must be $15,000.

When notarizing a circulator's affidavit, you may charge what fee?

There is no fee for this notarization.

What happens if you fail to file your bond and oath on

time?

Your commission is void, and you need to complete a new application and pay $20 to reapply.

If you don't notify the Secretary of State about a name or address change, the fee is how much?

The fine is $500.

What additional duties is a California notary allowed to do?

They are allowed to take depositions and affidavits.

A first-time notary applicant must be what to get a commission in the state of California?

The individual must be at least 18 years old, pass the exam and be fingerprinted.

A non-attorney notary who is bonded and qualified as an immigration consultant may charge $10 for what services?

For completing a person's immigration application, for oaths and affirmations and for signatures on a Jurat.

How often does a notary need to take the exam if they are seeking reappointment?

A notary must retake the exam every 4 years when seeking reappointment.

What are all notary actions in the state of California?

Proof of Execution, Jurat, Oath of Office, Acknowledgement.

What must a notary do when changing a business

address to a new county in California?

They must notify the Secretary of State of the address change.

All appointed persons must complete what?

At least six hours of study.

A notary must meet what qualifications?

The notary must be a resident of California.

Notary Exam Test Taking Tips

When it comes to taking any exam, there are certain things you can do to increase your chances of passing the test. So consider the following tips when taking your notary exam, so you are able to pass your exam.

• When taking the test, it is important to stay relaxed and have a positive attitude.

• Maintain focus on your own test and not the test of others around you.

• Take the time to determine the concept that the question is testing.

• After reading the question, come up with a likely answer in your head and then read the potential answers. This helps to avoid getting sidetracked or confused by the choices provided on the test.

• Look for any overriding rules; this can be helpful when faced with word problems and scenarios.

• If you are faced with a scenario, you should take a moment to determine who the notary is in the scenario.

• Always choose the best answer. Use a process of elimination from the choices given and then choose the best answer.

• If you aren't completely sure of the answer to a question, then skip it for the moment. Sometimes other questions in the test will help you answer a question. Just make sure you come back to answer the question. An unanswered question is always going to be wrong, but taking a random guess will give you at least a 25% chance of getting a correct answer.

• Always choose the answer that is most whole and complete, which means it can stand on its own.

• Always check for keywords in the question, such as except, all, not, all except and other similar keywords. Read the test question once to look for these keywords and note and/or circle them. Then re-read the question. Then look at all potential answers before making your final choice.

• Look for all of the above and/or none of the above answer choices. If you are certain one statement is true, then don't choose none of the above as an answer, or if you know a statement is false, then don't select all of the above as an answer.

• Avoid reading into the question. Answer only what the question asks of you. Something may be correct or incorrect, but is that what the question is asking?

• If the question names a specific document, then determine any special conditions and/or limitations that pertain to that document, such as those listed in our study guide earlier.

• Often, the correct answer is going to be the choice

with the most information.

• A positive choice is often going to be more true than a negative choice.

• Always ask yourself if the answer makes sense and covers the whole problem.

• When all else fails, go with your gut instinct when choosing an answer.

So now you hopefully know what a notary job entails and have seen why going this route is a good idea for you. Then hopefully, we have shown you what you are likely to need to know for a notary exam. Finally, take the time to go through the practice tests as often as possible until you are ready to take the test. Then use the tips at the end of this book to help you pass your notary exam on the first try and start your new job.

Part 2: Must-Know Information to Pass the California Notary Exam

Even though the California Notary Handbook is available FREE online, we have summarized the important points that frequently are asked on the exam. The present summary is more like a last-minute review and will help you enormously with the important facts that you need to know.

The Application Process

Qualifications to Become a Notary in California

To become a notary in California, all applicants have to meet the following requirements:

• Legally reside in California

• Satisfactorily complete a course study approved by the Secretary of State

• Pass a background check

- Be at least 18 years of age

- Pass the Written exam

- Applicant must also submit a 2 x 2-inch color passport photo

---

Fingerprints & Convictions

Even if the notary has been in commission without a break for many years, fingerprints need to be submitted for a background check.

Do all convictions disqualify a person from becoming a notary?

In general, past convictions usually make it almost impossible to become a notary in California. However, this also depends on the type of crime, and the ultimate decision rests with the Secretary of State. Petty theft or trespass may not be a big deal, but fraud, DUI, or perjury are unlikely to persuade the Secretary to grant a commission. Whatever the case, it is vital that the applicant disclose all past convictions, even those where he or she was found not guilty. Finally, even if the conviction was several decades ago, it needs to be disclosed. Failure to disclose will result in the rejection of the application.

As part of the background check, only candidates who pass the exam will be required to submit fingerprints prior to being appointed as a notary.

All applicants must disclose all arrests, trials, and convictions. Even if the conviction was dismissed, it must be disclosed. In general, having a conviction may result in the cancellation of the application. However, the ultimate decision depends on the Secretary of state and the type of crime. For all serious offenses, no individual is granted a commission.

Applicants do have the right to appeal if there is a denial.

Notary Public Education

1. All applicants must take a 6-hour course that is approved by the Secretary of State.

2. No matter how many prior commission terms the individual has held, the 6-hour course study is mandatory.

3. A NP who is currently active and has already taken the 6-hour course will need to take the 3-hour course and pass it before a reappointment can be made.

4. The 3-hour course is only for NPs who are applying for a new commission before their present commission has expired.

5. If the commission has expired, the individual has to take the 6-hour study course and pass it.

6. All study courses are approved by the Secretary of State.

Qualifying for Practice as a Notary

1. After the commission is issued, the individual has 30 calendar days to take and subscribe to the oath of office and file a $15K surety bond with the county clerk's office.

2. The commission cannot be activated until the bond and oath are filed.

3. The filing of the oath has to occur in the county where the notary will remain in practice.

4. Failure to file the oath and bond within 30 days will result in an inactive commission.

Notary Public Bond

1. State law requires that all notaries file an official surety bond in the amount of $15K before their commission is activated. This notary bond is not an insurance policy but only provides limited funds for claims made against the notary.

2. The notary is responsible for maintaining insurance against personal liabilities (i.e., negligence or misconduct against clients).

Geographic Jurisdiction

1. Once the commission is valid, the notary can provide notarial services in any county in the State

2. When filling out the certificate, the notary public can state in which county the notarial act was performed.

Practice of Law

1. The state law is clear- notaries in California are prohibited from performing any legal activities, including giving advice and opinions.

2. In addition, Notaries are not allowed to draft or certify legal documents.

3. The best advice is to refer the client to a bona fide lawyer.

Appointment and Commission; Jurisdiction

1. All notary appointments are made by the Secretary of State

2. Notaries can work in any county in California

Notary Qualifications

1. Be a legal resident of the state.

2. Be at least age 18

3. Satisfactorily completed the 6-hour course of study.

4. Pass the written exam.

5. Submit fingerprints as part of a background check.

6. Submit a colored photograph 2 x 2 inches for the application.

7. Disclose all arrests and convictions.

8. The course study is usually approved by the Secretary of State. Any provider of education who violates the regulations adopted by the Secretary is subject to a civil penalty of $1,000 and pay restitution.

Term of Office

The notary commission is of 4 years duration. To continue on as a notary, the individual has to retake the study course approved by the Secretary of State

Cancellation of Commission

1. The Secretary of State has the authority to cancel the commission of a notary public for a variety of reasons,

including failure to pay fees.

2. A written notice will be sent to the notary asking why the fees have not been paid. A second notice 20 days later will have a written notice of cancellation, and the cancellation shall thereupon be effective.

Powers of Attorney - Certifying

A notary public can certify copies of powers of attorney. When a notary certifies a copy of a power of attorney, it has the same legal effect and force as the original power of attorney.

Note: It is important for the notary to beware that the notary's signature and public seal cannot be printed onto a notary document if the correct notary terminology is not used.

Notarization of Incomplete Documents

If the document appears incomplete or has missing pages, the notary public should not notarize the document. It is perfectly legal to refuse the notarization of incomplete documents.

Making edits to the Notarized Documents

1. There are no provisions in the law that permit notaries to make edits to notarized documents after the notary act is complete.

2. The general rule is that the notary should start the process all over again. Making edits of any type is not permitted.

3. Even if the edit is minor, the notary can be charged with a crime.

Certified Copies

1. A notary can only certify copies of power of attorney

2. Certified copies of death, birth, or marriage can only be made by appointed registrars and county recorders

Notary Public Seal

1. A notary public seal is mandatory in California.

2. The seal has to be kept in a locked and secure place at all times; it has to be under total control by the Notary public.

3. The notary seal should not be surrendered to the employer even if he or she paid for it.

4. The notary seal cannot be given to any other person.

5. The seal should clearly reveal, when embossed,

impressed, stamped, or affixed to a document, the notary name, the words notary public, the name of the county where the oath and bond were issued, and the date of expiration of the commission.

6. All seals now have a sequential ID number

7. All notary acts have to be authenticated with the seal.

8. The seal should only be used for notarial acts and services.

9. The circular seal should not have a diameter of more than 2 inches.

10. The rectangular seal should not be more than one inch in width and 2.5 inches in length.

11. At all times, the seal has to be kept in a secure and locked area and in full control of the Notary.

12. The seal is the exclusive property of the Notary and should not be surrendered to the employer, even if he paid for the seal.

13. In the event the Notary resigns or is terminated, the seal has to be destroyed. There are specific ways of destroying the seal, and details can be obtained from the Secretary of State.

Precautions

1. A notary seal is not to be duplicated, sold, or manufactured unless authorized by the Secretary of State.

2. Each notary seal will have the sequential ID number etched onto it.

3. The NP will only be able to purchase a new notary seal from the vendor after submitting a certificate of authorization (See below)

Apply for a certificate of authorization for a new seal if the old one is damaged or not working.

1. The certificate of authorization is issued by the Secretary of State. With this certificate, the NP can obtain an official notary seal.

2. When the certificate of authorization is presented to

a vendor or manufacturer, he or she will provide an official seal. The vendor will check the sequential identification number on the certificate.

3. The vendor will retain the copy of the certificate of authorization and then submit it to the Secretary of State for record-keeping

4. If the notary seal is misplaced, lost, damaged, etc., this should be reported to the secretary of State immediately. Within five days, the secretary will issue a certificate of authorization for a replacement seal.

Notary Seal Requirements

1. The notary seal must be photographically reproducible.

2. The words 'notary public' must appear on the seal.

3. The name of the notary public must be visible.

4. The county where the oath of office and bond were issued should be stated.

5. The expiration date of the NP's commission should

be visible.

6. The Sequential ID number assigned must be visible.

7. The seal can be circular or rectangular.

8. The circular seal cannot have a diameter of more than 2 inches.

9. The rectangular seal will have a width of one inch and a length of 0.5 inches. The borders may be milled or serrated.

10. If the notary seal is illegible, the document may be rejected.

11. The seal should not be placed over any printed items or signatures.

12. Subdivision maps are drawn on materials that do not usually accept a stamp ink pad and thus can be notarized without a seal.

13. The notary seal is only to be used for notarial acts.

14. If the notary seal is not kept in a secure location,

the crime is a misdemeanor.

15. When the notary public commission expires or is not valid, the seal must be destroyed to prevent fraudulent use by others.

Identification of Signers and Witnesses

1. When completing a certificate of acknowledgment or a jurat, the notary public must identify the signer of the document. The failure to identify signers is often the major complaint against notaries.

2. Identity is usually established when and if the notary public is presented with satisfactory evidence of the signer's identity.

3. "Satisfactory Evidence" usually refers to the absence of any evidence/information that would lead a reasonable individual to believe that the person is not who he or she claims to be. In such cases, the notary must utilize (A) identification papers with photos or (B) take an oath from a single credible witness, or (C) take the paths of two credible witnesses.

Identification Documents

The notary public may use any number of documents to identify the signer, and they include the following:

1. The ID has to be issued within five years and can be used even if it currently expired (as long as it is no more than five years)

2. A US passport

3. ID card from the California Dept of Motor Vehicles

4. Inmate ID that has been issued by the Dept of

Corrections and Rehabilitation

5. Any photo ID issued by law enforcement if the inmate is in custody.

6. Any consular ID that may be a passport or citizenship certificate

7. Driver's license from Canada or Mexico or from another US state

8. US military ID card

9. Employee ID cards

10. ID issued by the tribal government

No matter what ID is used, the Notary must record the facts about the ID in the journal, including who issued it, date of expiration, serial number, date of issue, etc.

Oath of a Single Credible Witness

1. Sometimes, the Notary may use an oath of a single credible witness to identify the signer

2. The single credible witness is usually personally known to the Notary

3. The Notary must still obtain some type of ID to establish the identity of the single credible witness

4. The credible witness must swear under oath that the signer of the document is the individual named in the document

5. The credible witness also personally knows the signer, and the signer does not possess any ID documents

6. The credible witness should not be named in the document and not have any financial interest with the signer

7. The credible witness must sign the notary journal and state what type of document is being signed

Oaths of Two Credible Witnesses

1. The Notary may use the oath of two credible witnesses to identify the signer.

2. The two credible witnesses may not know the

Notary.

3. First, the IDs of the two credible witnesses have to be verified.

4. The two credible witnesses need to swear under oath that the person signing the documents is the person named in the document.

5. Both credible witnesses have to sign the Notary's journal.

6. The Notary must include all details in the journal regarding the ID verification and sign-in process.

Notary Public Journal

1. NPs must keep a notary journal, and all notarial acts must be recorded in this journal

2. The journal has to be kept in a locked and secure area

3. The Notary will maintain an active sequential journal for the notarial duties.

4. The notary journal will be kept in a locked and secure area- failing to secure the journal can result in administrative action by the Secretary of State.

How to Retire a Journal

Resignation, disqualification, or removal of Notary - what to do with the journal?

1. If, for any reason, the NP resigns, is removed from office or is disqualified and there is no reappointment within 30 days, the Notary is responsible for delivering all notary papers to the clerks' office within 30 days.

2. Willful failure to deliver the notary papers can result in a misdemeanor that also has a monetary penalty.

3. If the Notary dies, then the personal representative of the deceased should notify the Secretary of State and deliver the notary records.

4. After ten years after the day of deposit with the county clerk, if there are no requests for these records, they will be destroyed as ordered by the court.

Journal Contents

When recording notarial acts in the journal, the following should be included:

1. Time, date, and the type of each official notarial act

2. The character of each document acknowledged, affirmed, proved or sworn to before the Notary public.

3. Signature of every individual whose document is notarized.

4. Statement of how the identity of the person making the acknowledgment or taking path was made-satisfactory evidence

5. What type of paper ID was used to identify the person taking the oath or acknowledgment

6. May use a Single Credible Witness personally known to the NP who will sign the journal or use two credible witnesses

7. Will state the fee in the journal

8. If the notarized document is a quitclaim deed, deed, deed of trust, or power of attorney, a right thumbprint is required in the journal. If the right thumbprint is not available, you may use a left thumbprint- If you cannot use a fingerprint, the Notary must explain why in the

journal

9. If the journal is lost, stolen, damaged, or misplaced, the NP must notify the Secretary of State IMMEDIATELY- the notification should include the number of journal entries, commission number, commission expiration date, and if available, a photocopy of the police report.

10. If a client makes a request for a copy of the journal, the NP must respond within 15 days. The photocopying charges should not be more than 30 cents per photocopy.

11. The journal is the exclusive property of the Notary.

12. The journal is not to be surrendered to an employer, even if the latter paid for it.

13. If the Notary has done something illegal, then the government can ask to review the journal.

14. If the Notary willfully fails to maintain the journal- this is a misdemeanor.

15. When the Notary's commission expires, he or she must deliver the journal to the county clerk's office.

Failure to do so can result in a misdemeanor and civil penalties in case any person is harmed by this action.

Acknowledgment & Jurat

1. The form most frequently completed by the notary public is the certificate of acknowledgment.

2. The notary will usually certify that the signer physically appeared before him/her and that the singer acknowledged executing the document.

3. The journal also needs an entry about the acknowledgment and that it was based on satisfactory evidence.

4. If the ID was based on the oath of one credible

witness known to the notary, the journal must contain the signature of the witness, including the types of documents used to establish his or her identity. Details about the type of ID document, date of issue, and expiration must also be recorded in the journal.

5. If the ID was based on the oath of two credible witnesses, the notary must have satisfactory evidence about their identity. Again all the details about IDs must be recorded in the journal.

6. If the notary willfully makes false statements while completing the certificate of acknowledgment, he or she can be liable for civil penalties and administrative actions. The civil penalty can be associated with a fine of $10K.

7. A notary public is permitted to complete a certificate of acknowledgment in another jurisdiction or state in the country on documents that have been filed in the other jurisdiction or another state on the condition that the notary is not required to certify or determine that the document signer's status or perform a certification or determination that is not permitted under the law in California.

Facts to Know

1. California law does not have a provision where a notary can edit, cross out, or delete any words on the notary documents.

2. One can also not attach an acknowledgment to the document, especially when the signer was not physically present.

3. Finally, a notary seal cannot be affixed to a notary document without the use of proper notarial terminology.

Jurat

1. The jurat is the second most completed form or notary action by the notary public.

2. The jurat is easily recognized by the presence of the following terminology on the form that include "Subscribed and sworn to (or affirmed)."

In the jurat, the notary public certifies:

1. That during the signing, the signer was physically present on that day

2. That the signer signed the document in front of the notary

3. The notary administered the oath or affirmation.

4. The identity of the signer was confirmed.

5. The notary has to administer an oath or affirmation when executing a jurat.

6. Will use satisfactory evidence to determine the ID of the person executing the document

7. The Secretary of State has the power to appoint public school district employees and military and naval personnel to act as notaries on behalf of the government.

8. The term of appointment will cease when these individuals cease to be employees of the school or military.

9. The commanding office will notify the Secretary of State when the individual's employment is terminated.

10. When these individuals render public service, there are no fees collected.

Additional Considerations

A jurat cannot be affixed to a notary document if the signer does not take the oath, was not physically present, or signed in the presence of the notary.

Similarly, a notary seal and signature cannot be affixed to the document if proper notarial terminology is not used.

Proof of Execution by a Subscribing Witness

What is a Subscribing witness?

A subscribing witness is an individual who hears or sees writing executed or hears it acknowledged and, at the request of the NP, signs his name as a witness.

Subscribing Witness 101

1. If the principal individual has signed the document but does not physically appear before a notary, another

individual can appear on behalf of the principal and prove that the principal signed the document.

2. The person who vouches for the principal indicating that he was the person who signed the document, is called a subscribing witness.

3. However, a subscribing witness's execution is usually not permitted with instruments like the quitclaim deed, power of attorney, quitclaim deed, grant deed, deed, mortgage, security agreement, deed of trust, or any other tool that deals with real estate.

Subscribing Witness Requirements

1. Subscribing witness has to take an oath that the principal was the person who signed the document and that he or she knows the principal.

2. The subscribing witness must state under oath that he saw the principal sign the document.

3. The subscribing witness also has to say under oath that he or she was requested by the principal to appear as a witness to the document signing.

4. The notary must establish the ID of the subscribing witness.

5. The subscribing witness must sign the notary journal; the notary must state which document was signed and the type of ID used.

6. The ID of the subscribing witness has to be established by an oath of a credible witness who personally knows both the notary and principal.

Signature by Mark

There will be times when the signer is unable to sign, and that individual will have to use a Mark.

Requirements for notarizing a signature by mark:

1. The individual signing with a mark has to be identified by the notary with satisfactory evidence.

2. The signer's mark must be witnessed by two individuals. The witnesses only very that the individual is using a mark to sign the document

3. The IDs of the two witnesses do not require verification, nor do these witnesses have to sign in the notary journal.

4. However, if the two witnesses are acting in the capacity of credible witnesses, then their identity must be established, and they also have to sign the journal.

5. The signer must also include the mark in the notary journal; this act must also be witnessed by the individual.

Fees

General Guidelines

1. The government has set a cap on the maximum amount of fees that notaries can charge for their services.

2. However, the notary can charge less for his or her services

3. All fees must be recorded in the journal

4. Even if no fees are charged, this must still be

recorded in the journal

5. Notaries should not collect fees from veterans to certify any type of veteran document

6. The notary should not charge fees to notarize any voting material like mail ballot identification envelopes

---

Specific Fees

1. Proof of a deed, Acknowledgment or another related instrument, including the seal and the writing of the certificate- $15 for each signature

2. Oaths/Affirmations Administering an oath or affirmation to one person -$15

3. Executing the jurat, including the seal, $15

4. Deposition Services All services rendered in connection with taking a deposition- $30

- Administering the oath to the witness $7

- Certificate to the deposition- $7

5. Voting Materials Notarize signatures on vote-by-mail ballot identification envelopes or other voting materials- $0

6. Powers of Attorney Certifying a copy of a power of attorney $15

7. No fees for any veteran documents, including pension, compensation, allowance, etc

8. Notarization of immigration forms has a fee cap of $15 per individual

Precautions for Charging Fees

1. To prevent overcharging, California law has strict laws on maximum fees that can be charged by notaries for their services.

2. The fees should not exceed the fees recommended by the Secretary of State.

3. There is a $15 fee for taking an acknowledgment, proof of a deed, or other tools, and this also includes writing the certificate and applying the seal.

4. $15 fee for administering an affirmation or an oath and executing the jurat, including the seal

5. All services related to taking a deposition- $30. In addition, $7 for administering the oath to the witness and $7 for the certificate of deposition

6. There is no fee to notarize signatures on vote-by-mail ballot ID enveloped or all other voting material.

7. For certifying Power of attorney, $15

8. No fee should be charged to all Veterans for notarizing applications for allotment, pension, compensation, allowance, insurance, or any other veteran benefit.

Surety Bond

1. All appointed notaries have to execute an official surety bond of $15,000.

2. Before starting the term of the commission, the NP must file an official bond and take an oath of office. This has to be done within 30 days of starting the commission term.

3. The oath and bond have to be in the office of the county clerk in the county where the NP is planning to practice.

4. The county clerk usually retains the oath of office for 12 months following the expiration of the commission term, after which the oath is disposed of or destroyed.

5. When a notary public transfers the place of business to another county, filing for a new oath of office and bond come with the same recording fees as before

6. If the surety decides to be released from the responsibility on account of notary-related issues, this can be done by making a written application to the superior court where the notary public is in practice.

7. The notice of the hearing is also sent to the Secretary of State.

Prohibited Activities

Illegal Advertisement

For illegal advertisement, the Secretary of State can suspend the notary for up to a year or revoke the commission. A second offense usually means permanent revocation of the commission.

1. When a notary posts any type of advertisement in a language other than English, he or she has to have a disclaimer saying that he or she is not a lawyer and can't give legal advice about immigration or any legal matter.

2. It is also mandatory that notaries list their fees for notarial services.

3. The ad may not be translated into Spanish, and it is prohibited to use the words notario or notario publico

4. A first offense for violation of this law can result in revocation or suspension of the notary commission. A second offense usually means permanent revocation of the public commission.

5. The general rule is that notaries in California are barred from promoting themselves as immigration specialists.

Acting on Immigration Documents

1. There is no law that prevents notaries from notarizing immigration documents.

2. However, there are strict laws on what a notary can and cannot do. The key is not to act as a lawyer or offer legal advice.

3. Only a registered lawyer is able to work as an immigration consultant.

4. When notarizing immigration documents, the notary cannot charge above the cap of $15 for each form. Only lawyers can charge more for their services.

Confidential Marriage Licenses

1. A notary public who wants to authorize confidential marriage licenses first needs approval from the county clerk where he or she resides.

2. Only after getting this approval can the notary perform authorization of the confidential marriages

3. In addition, for a notary public to perform the marriage ceremony, he or she must be authorized under the family code (e.g., minister, rabbi, or priest)

4. The county clerk does not approve all applications from notaries who want to authorize confidential marriages.

Grounds for Revocation and Suspension of Commission

1. The Secretary of State has complete authority to

refuse, revoke or suspend the commission of a notary public for specific reasons.

2. Common reasons for suspension or revocation include failing to disclose convictions on the application, misrepresentation, convictions- usually a felony, etc. In addition, failing to provide the Secretary with the requested information, charging excessive fees, failing to complete the acknowledgment, and failing to document notary acts in the journal are also reasons for the suspension.

3. Disqualification or suspension can also result if the notary does not comply with family or child support obligations.

Disciplinary Guidelines

The Secretary of State has published disciplinary guidelines. These disciplinary guidelines are not set in stone, and it all depends on the severity of the crime or illegal behavior.

1. If the notary is negligent or is charged with misconduct, he or she can be liable in a civil action if any

individual is harmed or injured.

2. The Secretary of State can refuse any appointment, revoke or suspend the commission of a notary charged with a crime.

3. Any conviction is incompatible with the duties of a notary.

4. The use of misleading or false advertising is another common reason why notaries run into trouble with the law.

5. Charging excess fees is a common reason for misconduct.

6. Any act of commission with an intent to benefit the notary or injure another person can result in a civil penalty.

7. Failing or not completing the acknowledgment at the time of the notarization is also a common reason why notaries are charged with a crime.

8. Executing a certificate that contains false information is a crime.

9. Failure to submit the journal to a peace officer is also a crime.

10. Failure to document in the journal is a crime.

11. Failure to have the thumbprint in the journal is also a crime.

Notaries, the Law and Protest

1. The general rule in California is that notaries should not get involved with immigration matters.

2. Even if a notary has expertise in immigration, there are fee limitations.

3. The notary cannot advertise himself as an immigration expert.

4. A notary can certify immigration papers but cannot give advice on legal matters.

5. The fee to certify immigration papers should be no more than $15 for each set of forms.

6. At no time should a non-bonded notary perform the services of an immigration consultant.

Outside Influence

1. Any individual who coerces or influences a notary public to perform improper notarial acts can be charged with a misdemeanor.

2. For outside violations, the prosecution can commence within four years after the discovery of the offense.

3. A person not qualified as a notary can be charged with a misdemeanor if he performs the actions of a notary or advertises himself as a notary.

4. Unlawful acts by a non-notary to deeds of trust on single-family residences can result in a charge of a felony.

Enforcement

1. If the Secretary of State or a peace officer believes that there is reasonable suspicion of a crime or violation of a notarial act, they can force the notary to hand over the journal and all related notarial material.

2. If the notary fails to keep the notary under his exclusive control, this can result in a misdemeanor.

3. Prosecution for this violation can be commenced within four years from the discovery of the offense.

4. If the notary gives any certificate that is not true, he can be guilty of a misdemeanor.

5. If the notary willfully states that material is true when in fact, it is false, he or she can be subject to a civil penalty of $10,000.

Protest; Noting for Protest

1. In simple terms, a protest when it comes to notaries is making a complaint that is public.

The notary may state emphatically and firmly when faced with implied doubt or, more often, following an accusation. In general, to make the protest, one must have sufficient information to back up the argument.

2. The protest has to identify and define the tool/instrument. In addition, the notary or the individual making the protest has to certify what the opponent/client has said. For example, the notary may not have accepted or dishonored a payment from the client for a specified reason.

3. The protest usually requires that the notice of dishonor be distributed to some or all of the parties concerned.

Miscellaneous Instances

Change of Address

1. If an NP makes a change of address, the secretary of state must be notified in writing within 30 days

2. Failure to notify can result in an infraction with a fine of $500

3. After a change of address, the NP must file for a new oath and bond

4. There is no fee for processing the change of address

Foreign Language

1. The NP can notarize a signature on a document in a foreign language, even if he or she is not familiar with the language, because the NP's function relates to the signature and not the contents of the document.

2. However, the NP should have some idea of which document is being notarized. If unable to identify the document, the NP must state that in the journal.

3. The document should never be notarized if it appears incomplete.

4. The use of interpreters is not recommended, as critical information may be lost in translation.

5. If there is a complete lack of communication with the client, referral to an NP who speaks the same language as the client is highly recommended.

Electronic Notarizations

1. NPs are allowed to perform notarizations on

electronic documents, but only if all the traditional paper-based notarial acts are met.

2. However, the signer must physically appear before the notary to obtain a jurat or an acknowledgment.

3. Non-physical presentation or video images will not do

Conflict of Interest

The notary should not certify documents for relatives and families because of conflicts of interest. California has strong community property law, and great care should be exercised in notarizing documents belonging to the spouse or domestic partner.

A notary may have a beneficial or financial interest in the following cases:

• If he or she is named as a principal to a financial transaction

• If he or she is named to a property transaction, grantor, beneficiary, mortgagee, mortgagor, grantee, trustee, trustor, vendor, lessor, vendee, or lessee.

In general, a notary does not have a beneficial or financial interest if he or she is acting in the capacity of an employee, agent, attorney, insurer, lender, or escrow holder.

If there is any doubt, the notary should consult with an attorney.

Notarization for a Friend

Even if the notary has known the friend or neighbor for many decades, a jurat cannot be executed, nor can the notary take an acknowledgment. Satisfactory evidence of the signer's identity is a must and should be recorded in the journal.

Name Change

1. When a notary public makes a name change, the secretary of state should be notified within 30 days.

2. At the same time, the NP should file a new oath for the office and file for a surety bond.

3. The NP will have to pay a recording fee for the name

change and filing for the oath.

4. If the NP makes a name change, the Secretary of State must be notified within 30 days by writing-usually certified mail.

5. Willful failure to notify the Secretary of state of the name change can result in an infraction punishable by a fine of $500

Must-Know Definitions

Felony: A crime that is usually associated with violence and far more serious than a misdemeanor. The victim usually suffers extensive harm or damage as a result of a felony. The punishment for a felony usually involves a large monetary penalty and/or incarceration.

Misdemeanor: is usually considered to be a lesser crime than a felony and a very common problem in society. An example of a misdemeanor includes filing false documents. Misdemeanors are usually punished with a monetary penalty and/or community service.

Infraction usually refers to infringement or violation, or breach of statutes. The act of infraction is minor, and hence the penalty is small. Typical examples of an infraction include speeding, parking overtime, or tailgating.

Wilful misconduct refers to action when an individual engages in improper or unlawful behavior in the workplace; the wrongful behavior is on purpose. To be considered wilful, there has to be an element of deliberate and intentional. The improper behavior may harm the employer indirectly or directly.

Negligence is said to occur when the individual does not exercise the level of care that someone of ordinary mentation would have undertaken when faced with similar circumstances. Negligence may consist of omissions or actions that deviate from the standard duty of care.

Forgery is the act of falsely altering, making, or changing a document with the intention of committing fraud. Forgery may include falsifying signatures on journal records and duplicating seals. If an NP commits forgery, the penalty may be up to 12 months in prison.

Perjury: people lie all the time, but when one lies under oath, it is called perjury. It is a very serious offense that carries serious penalties. Taking an oath is common in the notary profession. People who take an oath declare, testify or certify in the presence of a notary that they will tell the truth; however, lying after taking the oath is perjury. Perjury is punishable by imprisonment ranging from 2- 4 years.

Must-Know Fees and Penalties

Infraction: Penalty $500

- Failure to contact State re Name change

- Failure to contact State re Address change

Negligent Failure: Penalty $750

- Failure to obtain an ID

- Failure to complete Acknowledgment

- Failure to perform duties & Responsibilities

- Overcharging

Misdemeanor: Fine $1000

- Practicing Law, giving advice on legal matters

Willful Misdemeanor: Penalty: $1,500

- Wilful neglect of duties and responsibilities

- Illegal advertising related to immigration

- Failure to notify SOS regarding a damaged seal

- Making an unauthorized duplicate seal

- Using false notary terminology

- Conducting fraud and deceit

- Journals to CC

- Failing to keep the journal secure

Wilful Misdemeanor: Penalty: $2,500

- Failing to stamp thumbprint in journal

- Refusing to give the journal to a peace office

Felony: Penalty: $10,000

- Falsifying acknowledgment

- Failing to identify credible witnesses and not having their signature in the journal

Misdemeanors:

- Acting as a notary ($1,000)

- Falsifying notary words ($1,000)

- Coercing or forcing notary to do an illegal notary act ($1,000)

- Falsifying journal content ($1,000)

- Destroying or hiding the journal ($1,000)

Felonies:

- Acting as a notary on real estate matters ($10,000)

- Perjury or forgery- (Penalty is 2,3 or 4 years)

- Filing False documents ($75,000)

Practice Test 1

This is a comprehensive collection of questions for the California Notary exam. The only syllabus to read is the California Notary Public Guide, which is released each year. It contains all the relevant text needed to pass the exam. The exam is 60 minutes long, and there are 45 questions. There are 9 questions that do not count towards the score, so you need to answer 34 questions correctly. About 40% of the exam tests fundamental facts that notaries need to know. About 40% of the exam is strictly based on fines and types of punishment- this is a must-know. The exam focuses heavily on numbers that the notary should know. The questions are not straightforward but are asked in a scenario format. A passing score of 70% is required. Candidates who pass or fail the exam are usually notified by mail in 15 days.

The exam is not difficult, and all the material comes from the guidebook. The key is to practice as many questions as you can so that you get familiar with the different ways the questions are asked.

Our exam covers the entire guide released by the California Secretary of State (https://www.sos.ca.gov/notary/handbook). Questions have been asked on almost every topic in the guide.

1. To become a notary public in California, the applicant must meet which requirement?

a. Be an American citizen

b. Have at least a college degree

c. Have no more than one conviction

d. Be at least 18 years of age

Answer D

To become a notary public in California, the applicant has to meet all of the following requirements:

• Be at least 18 years of age

• Be a legal resident in the State

• Pass a background check

• Prior to taking the Notary exam, one must have satisfactorily completed a course of study approved by the

Secretary of State

• Pass the written exam, which has been approved by the Secretary of State.

2. Which of the following is not a criterion for becoming a notary for the first time in California?

a. Be at least age 18

b. Pass a background check

c. Pass the 3-hour study course approved by the secretary of state

d. Be a legal resident of the State

Answer C

All candidates who want to be a notary must satisfactorily pass a 6-hour study course approved by the Secretary of State.

3. To take the notary exam, one must first take a study course approved by the Secretary of State. What is the duration of this course?

a. 2 hours

b. 4 hours

c. 6 hours

d. 12 hours

Answer C

Prior to taking the Notary exam, the applicant must have satisfactorily completed a course of study approved by the Secretary of State. The duration of this course is 6 hours

4. Prior to being appointed as a Notary Public in California, the applicant needs to:

a. Submit fingerprints

b. Have no debt

c. Have a job ready

d. Submit a DNA sample

Answer A

The Secretary of State requires fingerprints as part of the background check for all applicants. The fingerprint requirements are only sent to applicants who pass the notary exam.

5. At a minimum, to become a notary public in California, how many convictions can the applicant have?

a. 0

b. 1

c. 2

d. Less than 5

Answer A

All applicants are supposed to disclose any arrests,

trials, and convictions, including cases that have been dismissed. In general, even one conviction can result in the cancellation of the application. However, the Secretary of State decides on each case, and the more severe the crime, the less likely that the individual will be allowed to become a notary. Failing to mention past convictions or felonies results in denial of the application.

6. In general, if one becomes a notary public in Orange County, where else can the individual practice?

a. Practice limited to Orange County

b. Practice limited to Southern California

c. Practice limited to within 25 miles of present office

d. Any jurisdiction in the State

Answer D

A commissioned notary can practice in any jurisdiction in California. As long as the commission is valid, the notary can work anywhere in the State.

7. Which of the following offenses will not bar the applicant from becoming a notary public in California?

a. Hit and run

b. Practicing without a license in a profession where one is needed

c. Medicare fraud

d. Smoking medical marijuana

Answer D

In California, there are many cannabis laws that limit the use of this agent in the State. However, as long as one uses medical marijuana that has been obtained with a valid prescription and a bona fide clinic, there is no harm. However, notaries need to declare the use of medical marijuana and will need to prove how much they consume and why. The application can appeal the denial, which requires an administrative hearing process.

8. Which of the following reflects a Wilful misdemeanor?

a. Falsifying a journal entry

b. Destroying a journal

c. Committing perjury

d. Overcharging client

Answer A

When a notary makes a false entry into the journal, this is considered to be a wilful misdemeanor.

9. Which of the following statements about notarization is true?

a. A notary can notarize his or her own document only if it is an emergency

b. A notary can notarize his or her own document at anytime

c. A notary can notarize his or her own document if another notary is not readily available

d. A notary should not notarize any document where he is the signer

Answer D

The general rule in California is that notaries are not allowed to notarize any document where they are also the signer of the document-meaning that they cannot notarize their own signature.

10. Which of the following statements is true?

a. Only a few states permit remote officiating when the document signer is not present

b. If a few pages of a document are missing, the notary should just sign both the first and last page

c. If running out of time, the notary can sign the documents the next day

d. A notary can seal a blank notary certificate to speed up the process of notarization

Answer A

In the State of California, remote signing is not permitted. Only a few states permit remote notarization, and they include Michigan, Minnesota, Montana, Texas, and Virginia. In California, the individual has to be physically present for the sign-in process. Further, a notary should never sign a document that has missing pages. The document to be notarized has to be dated on the same day as notarization, and the notary cannot sign a blank notarial certificate.

11. Which statement is false about the course that the notary public is required to take prior to the test?

a. The secretary of State usually approves a study course

b. The duration of the study course is 6 hours

c. All applicants must satisfactorily pass the study

course

d. The study course is not a requirement for those who already have held prior commissions in the past

Answer D

Prior to being appointed as a notary, all applicants must satisfactorily complete a 6-hour course approved by the Secretary of State. This requirement is a must, irrespective of how many notary commissions one has held in the past.

12. If the notary wilfully makes a duplicate of the notary seal without approval from the Secretary of State, he or she can be guilty of an:

a. Infraction

b. Negligent failure

c. Misdemeanor

d. Felony

Answer C

Making a duplicate of a notary seal is an illegal act that can result in a misdemeanor.

13. In general, where does the individual who wishes to practice as a notary public take the oath?

a. In the capital of the state

b. Where he or she took the exam

c. In the county of business practice

d. In any part of the State

Answer C

The oath filing has to occur in the county where the NP will remain in business.

14. Every notary public who wants to practice in California has to file an official surety bond of $15,000.

What is the purpose of this bond?

a. It is an insurance policy

b. It will provide limited funds for any claims against the NP

c. Will protect the State against any errors by the notary

d. It will provide funds for travel and other administrative matters

Answer B

The surety bond will provide limited funds for any claims made against the notary. Overall, the notary public will remain legally liable to the full extent for any damages or negligence during the course of his or her duties.

15. Wilful failure to provide a peace officer with your thumbprint can result in a civil penalty of:

a. $250

b. $500

c. $1,500

d. $2,500

Answer D

If a notary refuses to provide a peace officer with a thumbprint, this can result in a hefty civil penalty of $2,500.

16. Once a commission is issued, how long does the individual have to take the oath of office?

a. Seven days

b. Twenty-five days

c. Twenty days

d. Thirty days

Answer D

After the commission is issued, the individual has 30 days from the beginning of the term prescribed in the commission to take and subscribe to the oath of office.

17. What is a true statement about a notary public's (NP) practice in California?

a. The NP can prepare a legal document

b. NPs can offer advice on legal matters

c. NPs can draft a legal document like a house deed

d. NPs should refer clients to lawyers

Answer D

The law is strict on the function and responsibilities of NP in California. They are also not to act like lawyers or give out legal advice. Notaries are not even allowed to prepare legal documents. If faced with any legal scenario, the best advice is to recommend the client to a lawyer.

18. In general, prior to practice, how much surety bond should the notary file with the county clerk's office?

a. $2,500

b. $5,000

c. $10,000

d. $15,000

Answer D

There are several package deals of surety bonds that come with or without errors & omissions. The basic bond amount is $15,000 and costs $50. The California notary bond is designed to protect the citizens of the State from any errors that the notary may cause during the notarial duties. The commission does not become active until the individual has taken the oath and fulfilled the bond requirements.

19. What is true about the notary public seal?

a. Having a notary seal is not a requirement in California

b. The notary public seal can be borrowed from a colleague for temporary use

c. The notary public seal can be made into a duplicate

d. NPs in California are required to have a notary public seal

Answer D

All notaries should have a notary public seal in the State of California. This seal is not to be borrowed, lent, or duplicated. It belongs to the notary and must be safely stored.

20. In general, where does the individual who wishes to practice as a notary public take the oath?

a. In the capital of the state

b. Where he or she took the exam

c. In the county of business practice

d. In any part of the State

Answer C

The oath filing must take place in the county where the notary will be practicing. This address must match the one when the notary filed the application.

21. If a notary files false documents, this is considered to be a:

a. Misdemeanor

b. Felony

c. Negligent failure

d. Infraction

Answer B

In general, filing false documents is considered to be a felony.

22. A notary public already holds a current commission and has already completed a 6 hours study course and passed it. But the rules state that these individuals still need to complete an approved study course of what duration?

a. 1 hour

b. 2 hours

c. 3 hours

d. 4 hours

Answer C

All notaries need to satisfactorily pass the study course. For first-timers, this study course approved by the Secretary of State is 6 hours. Once active, for renewal, the notary needs to pass a 3-hour study course satisfactorily. This three-hour refresher course is necessary to satisfy the education requirement if the notary public is applying for a new commission before their current commission has expired. If the notary public's commission has expired, the individual must satisfactorily complete a six-hour notary public education course before being appointed for another term, even if the individual has already once satisfactorily completed an approved six-hour course for a previous commission. All courses are reviewed and approved by the Secretary of State; the material in these courses is what candidates must know to pass the written exam.

23. What is the geometry and dimension of a notary public seal?

a. Circular and not over 2 inches in diameter

b. Square with 2-inch sides

c. Triangular with 1.5-inch sides

d. Hexagon with a diameter of 2 inches

Answer A

The notary seal can be either circular or rectangular. The circular seal has a diameter of 2 inches. The rectangular seal is not more than one inch in width and two and one-half inches in length, with a serrated or milled-edged border.

24. When a notary public overcharges clients, he or she is guilty of:

a. Felony

b. Misdemeanor

c. Infarction

d. Negligent failure

Answer D

The State is very strict on what notaries charge. To prevent overcharging, there are standardized fees published that notaries have to abide by. Overcharging can result in charge of negligent failure.

25. Once a notary public has obtained a seal, how should the seal be stored?

a. With the secretary

b. Be kept in the office drawer

c. Should be with the NP at all times

d. It should be in a safe and secured locker

Answer D

The notary is responsible for safeguarding the seal. It has to be kept in a safe and secure place- preferably locked.

26. After 30 years of working as a notary public for a private insurer, a 65-year-old decides to retire and move back to his farm. What should he do with his notary public seal?

a. Give it back to the insurer

b. Send it back to the Secretary of State

c. Give it to a colleague who is just starting a career as an NP

d. Keep it

Answer D

When the notary decides to retire his commission, the notary still remains his property. It should not be discarded, given to the employer, or sent back to the county clerk's office. Even if the employer paid for the seal, it should not be returned to that person.

27. In general, according to the Secretary of State, it may not be possible to stamp the notary seal on the following:

a. Certified copies

b. Investment documents

c. Loan documents

d. Subdivision maps

Answer D

With a few exceptions, the notary seal is often applied to most documents. However, subdivision maps are drawn on materials that usually do not accept a standard ink pad stamp. Thus, subdivision maps are often notarized without a notary seal.

28. For falsifying an entry into the Journal, the penalty is:

a. $500

b. $1,000

c. $2,000

d. $2,500

Answer D

The penalty for false entries into the Journal starts at $2,500. The Secretary of State can impose even more penalties depending on the situation.

29. If the notary public destroys the Journal, the penalty is:

a. Incarceration for a month

b. $2,000 fine and incarceration

c. $10,000 fine

d. Loss of commission

Answer C

The penalty for damaging or destroying the Journal is a $10,000 fine.

30. If a notary acts on real estate documents, this illegal act is considered to be a:

a. Misdemeanor

b. Infarction

c. Negligent failure

d. Felony

Answer D

Notaries are not permitted to act on real estate documents, and there are serious penalties for those who do so. If a notary acts on real estate documents, he or she can be guilty of a felony. The Secretary may even impose additional fines, depending on the seriousness of the case.

Practice Test 2

1. If the notary willfully fails to maintain the notary public seal under direct control, he or she may be guilty of a:

   a. Misdemeanor

   b. Wilful neglect

   c. Infarction

   d. Felony

Answer A

If a notary willfully fails to maintain the notary public seal under the direct and exclusive control, he can be charged with a misdemeanor. No unauthorized person is allowed to use or possess a notary seal belonging to another person.

2. Which of these is considered a misdemeanor?

a. A Notary public practicing law

b. Acting as a notary on real estate documents

c. Filing false documents

d. Committing forgery

Answer A

Notaries are not allowed to call themselves lawyers, give legal advice or pretend to be lawyers. The state takes this illegal act very seriously. Acting as a lawyer can result in a misdemeanor.

3. If a notary public commits perjury, the potential penalty in California is:

a. Incarceration for 2-4 months

b. Monetary penalty

c. Incarceration plus a monetary penalty

d. Any of the above

Answer D

When a notary commits perjury, the ultimate penalty is decided by the Secretary of State. The penalty may range from a monetary fine to incarceration or both. Perjury is a serious offense and has severe repercussions for the notary in terms of practicing commission again.

4. After 35 years in private practice, the notary public does not wish to renew his commission. How must the individual handle the notary public seal?

a. Destroy it

b. Hand it over to the Secretary of state

c. Return it to the employer

d. Store it in a safe

Answer A

When the notary public commission is no longer valid, the notary public seal must be destroyed to protect the notary public from possible fraudulent use by another.

5. The Certificate authenticating the identification of the individual signing the document is known as:

a. Deed

b. Jurat

c. Conveyance

d. Passport

Answer B

When the notary completes a certificate of acknowledgment or a jurat, he or she must also certify the identity of the signer of the document.

6. If the notary public's Journal is stolen, then he or she must notify the Secretary of State within?

a. Immediately

b. Three business days

c. Seven business days

d. At anytime

Answer A

If the Journal is lost, stolen, misplaced, or damaged, the notary must immediately notify the Secretary of State. The notification should include as much detail about the journal entries as one can remember.

7. If a client requests a copy of the transaction made in the notary public's Journal, the notary must usually respond within?

a. Three business days

b. Seven business days

c. Fifteen business days

d. Thirty business days

Answer C

In general, when a client requests a copy of the transaction made in the Journal, the notary should respond within 15 days. The client is supposed to provide details about the encounter and the type of document that was notarized.

8. The penalty for acting as a notary public on real estate papers is:

a. $500 fine

b. $750 fine

c. $1,000 fine

d. Suspension for three months

Answer B

The penalty for acting on real estate documents is $750.

9. A notary public's name is in a transaction stating that he will derive a financial gift. What should the notary do?

a. Proceed with the notarization

b. Not proceed with the notarization

c. Proceed with the notarization as long as the financial gift amount is less than $1,000

d. Consult with his lawyer first

Answer B

When there is a perceived or real conflict of interest, a notary should not proceed with notarization; this is especially true where the notary has been named as a beneficiary of a gift.

10. With regard to the practice of law, which statement is true?

a. Notaries are not allowed to practice law

b. Notaries can only offer advice on legal matters

c. Notaries can only offer opinions on legal matters

d. Notaries can only offer verbal advice on legal matters

Answer A

In general, notaries in California are not allowed to act as lawyers; neither can they give any advice or opinion on legal matters. Pretending to be a lawyer has serious repercussions for the notary.

11. A 69-year-old notary is about to retire. According to the Secretary of State, what should he do with his Journal?

a. Return it to the employer

b. Return it to the local county clerk

c. Keep it

d. Give it to his successor

Answer C

Like the notary seal, the Journal belongs strictly to the notary and should never be given to anyone, including the employer, even if the latter paid for any expenses. There are specific State rules that pertain to the Journal and what should be done once the notary commission has expired.

12. One becomes an official notary in California after:

a. Filling the oath

b. After filing the bond

c. After filing both the bond and oath

d. After passing the exam

Answer C

Passing the exam is just one step, but in order to be an official notary, the applicant must FIRST file for a bond and an oath with the county clerk's office.

13. The shape of the notary stamp may be?

a. Triangular

b. Circular

c. Hexagon

d. Square

Answer B

The notary seal is available as a circular or rectangular object. Notaries also need to know its contents and dimensions-see later.

14. In general, who is not allowed to notarize documents?

a. Grantor

b. Trustee

c. Lawyer

d. Paralegal

Answer B

In general, a trustee is now allowed to notarize documents because there may be a conflict of interest.

15. If the notary public willfully fails to maintain the notary journal, he or she may be guilty of a:

a. Infarction

b. Misdemeanor

c. Felony

d. Wilful neglect

Answer B

If the notary willfully fails to maintain the notary journal, he or she may be guilty of a misdemeanor.

16. Once the notary public commission is no longer valid, within what time must the individual deliver all the notarial documents to the local county clerk's office?

a. Three days

b. Seven days

c. 15 days

d. 30 days

Answer D

Once the notary public commission is not valid or expired, the notary must deliver all related documents to the county clerk's office within 30 days. Failing to do so can result in a misdemeanor.

17. In the State of California, notaries most frequently complete which form?

a. Certificate of acknowledgment

b. Loan document

c. Jurat

d. Power of attorney

Answer A

Notaries in Ca most often complete the Certificate of acknowledgment. This form certifies the following:

1. The signer was physically present, and his or her identity was verified

2. The signer acknowledged executing the document

18. If during the completion of the Certificate of acknowledgment, the notary is fully aware that some of the information is false, he or she can be subject to a civil penalty of:

a. $1,000

b. $2,500

c. $5,000

d. $10,000

Answer D

Completing a certificate of acknowledgment despite knowing that some or all the information may not be true is a serious criminal offense that leads to a monetary fine of $10,000. In addition, there are usually other administrative and civil penalties.

19. After completion of a notarial act, the new notary notices an error on the document. What is the correct way to go about this, according to the Secretary of State?

a. Make the edits on the document and cross out the error

b. Make the edits in the presence of a witness

c. Attach an addendum to the notarized document stating what edits you have made

d. Repeat the notarization process again

Answer D

In general, there are no provisions in the law that permit edits or corrections of a completed notarial act. If an error is discovered, the best advice is to redo the document again, including a new notarial act and a new journal entry.

20. A notary public in California can only certify copies of?

a. Birth certificate

b. Marriage records

c. Power of attorney

d. Death

Answer C

In general, a notary in California can certify copies of powers of attorney. Only the state registrar can certify copies of the birth certificate, marriage records, and death.

21. For notarizing an immigration form, a notary is only allowed to charge?

a. $7

b. $15

c. $30

d. Any amount

Answer B

When it comes to immigration forms, a notary can only charge $15 for each set of forms. Only when functioning as an attorney, can the fees be higher.

22. As a practicing notary in the State of California who wishes to advertise notary services, what is one major requirement by the Secretary of State?

a. That the notary is an American citizen

b. Notary has no prior convictions

c. That the advertisement is paid by a third party

d. Must add a statement in English that you are not a lawyer and do not give legal advice

Answer D

The law is clear when it comes to advertisements by notaries. Overall, ads are not recommended by the State. Plus, a notary can never advertise that he or she can offer advice on legal matters. If advertising, the notary must add a disclaimer that he or she is not a lawyer and cannot give legal advice.

23. If a notary public places an illegal advertisement stating that he/she can offer immigration advice, a first-time violation can result in:

a. Suspension of the commission

b. $1,000 fine

c. Need to take an ethical course

d. Redo the notary exam

Answer A

When a notary falsely advertises that he or she is a lawyer or can offer legal advice, a first-time offense can lead to revocation or suspension of the notary's commission. A second-time offense may lead to permanent revocation of the notary's commission. Notaries in California are not permitted to advertise that they have legal knowledge or can offer legal advice.

24. If you make a duplicate of your seal without approval from the Secretary of State, this illegal activity can result in a fine of?

a. $500

b. $750

c. $1,000

d. $1,500

Answer D

Making a duplicate of a seal is an illegal act, and the notary can face a monetary penalty of $1500.

25. If a notary advertises himself as an immigration specialist, this illegal activity can result in a fine of?

a. $500

b. $750

c. $1,000

d. $1,500

Answer D

Notaries in California should never call themselves immigration specialists if they have no prior expertise in that field. Acting as an immigration specialist is an illegal act that can easily cost the notary a fine of $1,500.

26. What fee should the notary charge to notarize a signature on the vote-by-mail ballot identification envelopes?

a. No fee

b. $7

c. $15

d. $20

Answer A

The state recommends no fees should be charged to notarize signatures on vote-by-mail ballot identification envelopes or, for that matter, any other voting items.

27. If the notary certifies a copy of a power of attorney, what is the amount of fee he/she can charge?

a. No fee

b. $7

c. $15

d. $20

Answer C

For certification of a copy of a power of attorney, the fee is set at $15.

28. What is the current status of notaries issuing confidential marriage licenses?

a. All notaries in California can issue confidential marriage licenses

b. Prior approval by the county clerk is required prior to approving a confidential marriage license

c. One does not have to be an authorized person to issue a marriage license

d. The county clerk usually approves all notaries who want to issue confidential marriage licenses

Answer B

Notaries who are interested in issuing confidential marriage licenses first need to write to the county clerk and get approval. Without this approval, the notary cannot issue a confidential marriage license. The clerk only grants a few approvals each year.

29. What is a false statement about fees that notaries collect?

a. There is a cap on fees that are established by the Secretary of State

b. A notary can charge less than the amount recommended by the State

c. The fee should not exceed the maximum amount stated by the State

d. If no fees are charged, this does not need to be

documented in the journal

Answer D

The Secretary of State has a published list of the maximum fees that notaries can charge for their services. The notary cannot charge more than the cap but can charge less. However, even if no fee is charged, it still must be recorded in the journal.

30. Which of the following is a false statement about notarizing a document in a foreign language?

a. In order to notarize, the notary should be able to communicate with the client to affirm the contents

b. Sometimes a referral to a notary that speaks the client's language is necessary

c. Always use an interpreter when faced with clients who speak another language

d. The notary still has to document the process in the journal

Answer C

There are times when the notary will have a client that speaks a foreign language. In order to notarize, the notary must be able to communicate with the signer. In general, an interpreter should not be used because vital information can be lost during translation. Sometimes it is best to refer the client to a notary who speaks his or her language.

Practice Test 3

1. Which statement is false about electronic notarizations in California?

a. A notary can perform notarization on documents electronically as long as all the paper-based notarial requirements are met

b. The individual must physically appear before a notary for a notarial act

c. A video image can be substituted instead of a physical presence

d. The individual must be physically present for a jurat

Answer C

California does not allow for electronic notarizations under current law. However, if all the traditional paper-based requirements are met, electronic notarization can be performed. But the individual must be physically present before the notary public. Video or a digital image will not do.

2. A new notary recently encountered a client who wanted to notarize a signature on a document written in Russian. What should he do?

a. Refuse notarization

b. Refer to a Russian notary

c. Can notarize as long as he is able to identify the document

d. Get the document translated into English first

Answer C

Just because a client speaks another language does not mean that the notary cannot notarize the documents. The key function of the notary relates to the signature and not the document contents. At the most basic level, the notary should be able to identify the type of document being notarized. The notary must be confident about what he is notarizing, and if that fails, referral to a Russian notary may be the best option.

3. During the process of notarization, the notary fails to identify a credible witness. What is the usual penalty for this incident?

a. Incarceration for two years

b. $2,000

c. $5,000

d. $10,000

Answer D

Failing to identify a credible witness is a serious violation and can lead to a $10,000 fine. The onus is on the notary to verify the identity of all witnesses and signers.

4. A client has brought in a scanned document that he wants to be notarized. What is the protocol?

a. All scanned documents can be notarized

b. All scanned documents can be notarized as long as they are legible

c. All scanned documents can be notarized as long they have an original signature

d. No scanned document can be notarized

Answer C

In general, scanned documents can be notarized as long as they have an original signature. The signature should be with an ink pen. On the other hand, a faxed or photocopied signature should never be notarized.

5. In order for a notary public to resign in California, within what time period should the notary documents be delivered to the county clerk?

a. Seven days

b. 14 days

c. 21 days

d. 30 days

Answer D

For those notaries who resign, the onus is on them to have the notary documents delivered to the county clerk's office within 30 days.

6. An applicant for a notary public has a past DUI conviction that happened more than 20 years ago. Is it necessary to disclose this conviction on the application?

a. Yes, all convictions should be disclosed

b. No, since it was a long time ago

c. As long as the record has been clean since then, there is no need for disclosure

d. Need to consult with a lawyer

Answer A

In general, the law is clear- all convictions, even those where the individual was not found guilty, have to be disclosed. Failure to disclose may mean the inability to become a notary in the state. The Secretary of State is the only person to determine who can be a notary following a conviction.

7. In general, in the state of California, the notary public test results are valid for what time period?

a. Three months

b. Six months

c. Nine months

d. 12 months

Answer D

After taking the test, the results are valid for 1 year from the exam date.

8. If an individual already holds a notary public commission, when should he or she take the test for

reappointment?

a. One month prior to the expiration of the current commission

b. Two months prior to the expiration of the current commission

c. Three months prior to the expiration of the current commission

d. At least six months prior to the expiration of the current commission

Answer D

The general recommendation is that one should take the exam at least six months before the expiration of the current term.

9. The notary's commission will expire in 2 months, and he needs to renew the commission. The state requires that he take a study course, that is?

a. 6 hours duration

b. 3 hours duration

c. No time limit

d. 1-hour duration

Answer B

If the commission is still active, the notary needs to take a 3-hour study course that has been approved by the Secretary of State.

10. Before a notary can start practice, what is the amount of bond that must be filed with the state?

a. $1,500

b. $5,000

c. $10,000

d. $15,000

Answer D

All notaries who want to practice first need to file for a surety bond of $15,000. This bond will provide limited funds in case of errors made by the notary.

11. A new notary places an advertisement claiming that he can offer advice on immigration matters. What is the penalty for this illegal action?

a. $500 fine

b. $1,000 fine

c. $1,500 fine

d. Loss of commission

Answer C

For violating the no advertisement rule on immigration matters and law, the penalty for a first-time offense is $1,500.

12. When a client makes a formal, solemn, declaration that specific statements he has made are true under the penalty of perjury, this is known as:

a. Affidavit

b. Affirmation

c. Deed

d. Pledge

Answer B

During affirmation, one makes a formal, solemn, declaration that specific statements he/she has made under the penalty of perjury are true.

13. For which offense can a notary receive a $1,500 fine and revocation of commission for 12 months?

a. Not reporting a lost seal

b. Failure to document in the journal

c. Signing a real estate document

d. Advertising services with the words 'notario publico'

Answer D

In general, notaries are now allowed to advertise their services or claim to be a lawyer. Further, the words "notario publico" or "notario" can not be used; if this happens, it can result in a monetary fine of $1,500 and revocation of commission for one year or more for the first offense. Second offense permanent revocation of your commission.

14. In which of the below scenarios can a notary charge a fee?

a. A Veterans Affairs life insurance form

b. The oath for the credible witness

c. A circulator's affidavit

d. A power of attorney

Answer D

In general, the notary can charge a fee to notarize a power of attorney. However, there is usually no fee for veterans and signing a circulator's affidavit.

15. A young client presents with a 2-page document for notarization. After examining the document, the notary notes that the last page is properly dated and signed, but the first page is torn with text missing. What should the notary do?

a. Complete the notarization

b. You should complete the notarization but only charge half the amount

c. You should not perform the notarization

d. You should fill in the missing text and then notarize

Answer C

When the document to be notarized is missing pages,

torn, damaged, or not legible, it is important not to notarize such documents. All signature pages need to be dated and signed properly. Incomplete documents should never be signed.

16. While in a hurry, a new notary knowingly notarizes a document that relates to real estate. This fraudulent activity can result in a:

a. Misdemeanor

b. Felony

c. Wilful neglect

d. Infarction

Answer B

Knowingly notarizing real estate documents is not allowed; doing so can result in a felony for a first-time offense. Repeated offenses can even lead to loss of commission.

17. The local county clerk has requested copies from the notary's journal. In general, how much can a notary charge for photocopying?

a. 2 cents a page

b. 5 cents a page

c. 10 cents a page

d. 30 cents a page

Answer D

Notaries can charge up to a maximum of 30 cents per photocopy.

18. If a notary retires and will no longer practice his commission, who is in charge of destroying the seal?

a. The notary himself

b. The Secretary of State

c. The local county clerk

d. The employer

Answer A

The notary seal is the property of the notary, and when the commission expires, it should not be discarded or given to anyone, not even to the employer. The Secretary of State has specific guidelines on how the notary should destroy the seal.

19. During the notarization of a power of attorney, the notary forgets to obtain a fingerprint from the client. What is the general penalty for this misadventure?

a. Incarceration for three months

b. $1,000 fine

c. $1,500 fine

d. $2,500 fine

Answer D

Failing to get a fingerprint from the client when notarizing a power of attorney is a serious offense. It can lead to a monetary penalty of $2,500.

20. According to the Secretary of State, what should the notary charge for a deposition certificate?

a. $7

b. $15

c. $30

d. $10

Answer A

For completing the certificate to a deposition, the notary charges are $7.

21. If the signer and notary public are not able to communicate because of a language barrier, the next step is to:

a. Cancel the sign-in

b. Use sign language to communicate

c. Use a language translator app on the smartphone

d. Use an interpreter

Answer A

In general, when the notary and the signer are not able to communicate, the sign-in should be canceled. The use of translators is not recommended, as one can lose the meaning of what is being translated. The best recommendation is to send the client to a notary who speaks the signer's language.

22. A junior notary just completed his first notarization. However, he later noticed that there was an error in the document. What should he do next?

a. Revise the error with a different ink

b. Revise the error but make sure it is dated

c. Use 'white out' ink to erase the error

d. Do not do anything

Answer D

Sometimes the notary may notice an error after the notarization process. The rule is simple; notaries should never make edits, corrections, or changes to an already notarized document. Alterations to a document can only be made during the execution of the notary process when the signer is still present. The notary should not do anything but has the option of redoing the entire process of notarization again.

23. A notary who has been working with an insurer for five years now finds a new job. What should he do with the seal?

a. Destroy it

b. Give it back to the first employer

c. Take it with him

d. Send it to the secretary of state

Answer C

A notary is allowed to practice his or her commission in the entire state. If a job change occurs, the notary should take the seal with him. The only thing one has to do is notify the Secretary of State of the address change. At the same time, you also need to request an oath of office. Later the county clerk will send you instructions for a new notary seal.

24. What fee does the state allow the notary to charge for taking an acknowledgment that includes a seal and a writing certificate?

a. $5

b. $10

c. $15

d. $30

Answer C

For taking proof of deed or an acknowledgment that includes a seal and writing of the certificate, the notary cannot charge more than $15 for each signature taken.

25. A colleague of yours who recently got married wants you to notarize his marriage license. What is the current status of such notarizations in California?

a. Not allowed

b. Only allowed if the marriage was in the state of California

c. Only allowed if both partners are present

d. Only allowed if the marriage was within one month

Answer A

In general, notaries in California are not allowed to notarize marriage certificates.

26. A colleague of yours resides in a different county and wants you to perform a notarization online. What is the current status of online remote notarization in the state?

a. Only permitted if there are no notaries in that specific county

b. Only permitted if it only pertains to the signing of a document

c. Not allowed

d. Only allowed if the individual lives in a rural area

Answer C

The State of California has not enacted/adopted notary statutes, regulations, or established standards and procedures for remote online notarizations. In general, the signer has to be physically present for the notarization process.

27. What is the maximum fee a notary can charge for

notarization in California?

a. $15

b. $20

c. $25

d. $30

Answer A

The fees for notarization are tightly regulated in California and are usually low. In most cases, a notary in California can only charge a maximum notary fee of $15 for each signature. This will include affixing the notary stamp, writing the certificate, and acknowledging the signature.

28. What does the term perjury mean?

a. It is the same as lying

b. The lying is pathological

c. Willfully telling an untruth in a court after having taken an oath

d. Lying that is documented on paper

Answer C

Perjury essentially is willfully telling an untruth in courts after having taken an oath. The intent is to deceive. People lie all the time, but in most cases, it is not after they have taken an oath.

29. How long is a notary public commission valid in California?

a. One-year

b. Two years

c. Three years

d. Four years

Answer D

In California, the notary public commission is valid for 48 months (4 years) after the date it was issued or from the time the candidate met the notary requirements before the County Clerk. The expiration date on every commission is visibly displayed.

30. To notarize a document, what should be the color of the pen?

a. Blue

b. Black

c. Red

d. It can be any color

Answer D

In the past, some people tried to argue that notary signatures can only be done with a blue or black ink pen. Fortunately this ridiculous bill was repealed. Today, a notary can use a pen of any ink to sign the documents.

Practice Test 4

1. Which of the following is not a duty of a notary public in California?

a. Administer oaths

b. Take depositions

c. Certify copies of power of attorney

d. Certify copies of real estate transactions

Answer D

In California, notaries are barred from notarizing real estate documents. It is considered illegal to notarize real estate documents by a notary, and one can face serious penalties for doing so.

2. If a notary public is found guilty of perjury, the punishment may include the following:

a. Two years incarceration

b. Three years incarceration

c. Four years incarceration

d. Any of the above

Answer D

Perjury is a serious crime punishable by imprisonment ranging from two to four years. The Secretary of State may also add additional punishment, such as loss of commission.

3. If a notary has committed forgery, the punishment is usually?

a. Suspension of commission

b. Up to a year in prison

c. $500 fine

d. Verbal warning

Answer B

Forgery is punishable by incarceration for not more than 12 months, but the Secretary of State may levy additional punishment depending on the seriousness of the crime.

4. Which of the following documents does the notary usually not notarize in California?

a. Loan documents

b. Passport applications

c. Legal affidavits

d. Death Certificates

Answer D

Death certificates are never notarized by notaries. Only approved individuals can certify death certificates.

5. What is a very common mistake made by notary publics across the State?

a. Failure to sign the document

b. Failing to apply the seal

c. Failing to require the signer to be present

d. Putting the wrong date

Answer C

A common mistake made by many notaries is the failure to have the signer present during the notarization process. It is the number one cause of misconduct against notaries in the State.

6. In general, when the document signer is not physically present, the notary:

a. Can still notarize as long as the witnesses are present

b. Cannot officiate

c. Can conduct a remote notarization

d. Can ask the signer to show up at a later date to confirm the signature

Answer B

The general rule in California is that if the document signer is not physically present, the notary should not officiate. Only five states allow for remote notarization, and California is not one of them.

7. Which of the following statements is false?

a. Once the notary act is complete, the notary is only allowed to make minor changes to the certificate

b. The notary should not complete a notarial certificate if he or she believes that the information is incorrect

c. The notary cannot certify the accuracy of the translated document

d. The notary is allowed to take the oath of the individual who swears that the translation is accurate

Answer A

Once a notary act has been completed, the notary is not allowed to make any edits to the document when the signer departs the office.

8. In general, what is the purpose of the notary's $15,000 public bond?

a. It is like an insurance policy

b. It protects the Notary against all liabilities

c. It protects the state of California against lawsuits

d. It partially protects the notary by providing a limited source of funds

Answer D

The surety bond of $15,000 only partially protects the notary from any claims that result from BAD notary acts. Overall, the notary is personally responsible for obtaining insurance to protect against liabilities that can occur as a result of negligence or misconduct.

9. Which of the following is not true about the notary public seal?

a. It reveals the date when the commission term started

b. The seal should be holographically reproduced when affixed to document

c. Contains the name of the county where the oath of office was issued

d. Contains the words 'Notary Public'

Answer A

The notary seal should leave a clear impression on the document, and all the elements should be visible. The seal should not be applied over any printed matter or the signature. The seal usually does not reveal when the commission term started. Documents may be rejected if the seal is improperly applied to documents.

10. When a notary has reasonable suspicion in the absence of any information that the individual is not the person he or she is claiming to be, this is known as:

a. Jurat

b. Fraud

c. Satisfactory evidence

d. Guilt

Answer C

Satisfactory Evidence refers to the absence of any evidence, information, or other related circumstances that would cause a reasonable individual to believe that the person asking for notarization is not the person he or she claims to be.

11. In general, a notary public can rely on identification documents provided it was issued within?

a. Past 30 days

b. The past year

c. Five years

d. 24-48 hours

Answer C

In general, identification documents need to be valid or have been issued within the past five years. One can use a driver's license, passport, an inmate ID card issued by the Dept of Corrections and Rehabilitation, or any other government-issued ID.

12. When using the oath of a single credible witness, which of the following statements is false?

a. The witness does personally not know the signer

b. The signer has no identification documents to verify his or her identity

c. The credible witness has no financial interests with

the signer

d. The credible witness is not named in the document that is being notarized

Answer A

When an oath of a single credible witness is used, the notary must first establish the identity of that individual. In most cases, the credible witness personally knows the signer. However, the credible witness should not have a financial interest, nor should he or she be named in the document.

13. The key difference between the oath of a single credible witness and two credible witnesses is:

a. The single credible witness personally knows the signer

b. The two credible witnesses personally know the notary

c. The single credible witness is usually related to the

signer

d. The two credible witnesses have a familial relationship with the signer

Answer A

In general, the single credible witness personally knows the signer. When it comes to two credible witnesses, the notary knows neither of them. In any case, the identity of the witnesses must be established before the sign-in can occur.

14. According to the Secretary of State, the law requires that the notary public journal be kept?

a. In the office at all times

b. Always be with the notary

c. Be kept in a locked and secure area

d. Be kept with the secretary

Answer C

The Notary Public Journal has to be kept in a safe and secure place that is locked. At all times, the notary must be in full control of the Journal. There are serious repercussions if the Journal is stolen, damaged, or destroyed.

15. If a form contains the wordings, 'Subscribed and sworn to', this indicates that the form is a:

a. Deed

b. Quitclaim

c. Jurat

d. Acknowledgment certificate

Answer C

The jurat is the second most common form that a notary completes on a regular basis. The jurat is easily recognized by the terminology "Subscribed and sworn to (or affirmed)" etched on the form.

16. If another individual appears on behalf of the principal to prove to the notary that the principal was the individual who signed the document, this person is called a?

a. Jurat

b. Single credible witness

c. Subscribing witness

d. Juror

Answer C

If another person appears on behalf of the absent principal to attest that the form was signed by the latter, this person is a subscribing witness

17. What fees does the state allow the notary to charge for affirmation to one individual and executing the jurat, including the seal?

a. $5

b. $10

c. $15

d. $30

Answer C

For affirmation or administering an oath and executing the jurat with the seal, the notary fees are capped at $15.

18. In general, what fee should the notary charge a US military veteran to notarize an application?

a. No fee

b. $7

c. $15

d. $20

Answer A

According to the Secretary of State, the notary should not charge any fees to Military veterans for the notarization of an application or any other veteran-related document.

19. In order to begin the term of the notary commission, all individuals must file an official bond and oath of office with the county clerk's office within what period of time?

a. Five business days

b. Ten business days

c. Fifteen business days

d. 30 business days

Answer D

In order to begin the prescribed commission, all appointed individuals must start working as a notary within 30 days of receiving the oath from the county clerk's office. If, for any reason, there will be a delay, the notary should write and explain the circumstances to the county clerk's office.

20. If the notary public is going to be notarizing a power of attorney, what is one requirement of the individual signing the document?

a. Individual must have two pieces of government-issued photo ID

b. A photographic image of the individual signing the document must be attached

c. The individual signing the document must provide a fingerprint

d. Each page has to be signed, dated, and notarized

Answer C

There are some documents that do require a thumbprint- these include a deed of trust, deed or a power of attorney. The notary must ensure that the individual places the right thumbprint in the journal. Not obtaining a thumbprint is a common complaint and associated with severe penalties for the notary.

21. Once the notary public commission is no longer active or valid, within what time must the notary deliver the notary journals to the country clerk's office?

a. Seven days

b. Fourteen days

c. 21 days

d. 30 days

Answer D

Once the notary commission is no longer active, the individual must return all the notary related documents to the local county clerk's office within 30 days; this is the same office where the notary had filed the oath and bond.

22. Which statement is false about the notary public

journal?

a. The pages should be numbered

b. Every notarial act must be documented

c. One has the option of maintaining the Journal in a digital format on a PC

d. The Journal must be kept in a locked and secure area

Answer C

The Notary Journal is an important document that must be kept in a safe and secure place; preferable in a locked area. At all times, the Journal has to be under control by the Notary. In California, the notary has to be paper based; so far the state has been reluctant to allow notaries to document notary activities on a PC. The reason is that PCs are regularly stolen and the software is hacked. Paper based journals appear to be more secure when stored properly.

23. The highest amount a notary in California charges clients is for?

a. Executing the jurat

b. Taking an acknowledgment

c. Taking a deposition

d. Noting a protest

Answer C

The maximum fees charged by a notary are for taking a deposition. A maximum sum of $30 is permissible.

24. For a notary in California, is a Notary Errors and Omissions Insurance policy mandatory?

a. Yes

b. No

c. Only if the notary has had a prior complaint from a client to the Secretary of State

d. Depends in which county you reside

Answer B

The Errors and Omissions insurance policy is not mandatory; there is no state law that requires notaries to have this policy. However, both the Secretary of State and the American Association of Notaries do recommend that notaries purchase this policy as it does provide solid protection against all sorts of liabilities.

25. For executing the jurat, a notary in California can charge what fee?

a. $10

b. $15

c. $25

d. $50

Answer B

The maximum fee that a notary can charge for

executing the jurat is $15.

26. A notary public has recently changed the location of his business. The change of address letter to the Secretary of State should be made within what time period?

a. Seven days

b. Fourteen days

c. 21 days

d. 30 days

Answer D

If the notary has changed the physical address of his practice, the Secretary of State needs to be notified within 30 days.

27. An individual in California has been an active notary public for more than three decades. Is he still required to take the initial 6-hour approved course of

study during renewal?

a. No need

b. No need as long as he has been practicing without any issues

c. Yes

d. Depends on the Secretary of State

Answer C

All notaries need to have the approved course of study, even those who have held previous commission terms.

28. What is the status of a notary journal requirement in California?

a. It is not mandatory to have one

b. Every notary must keep an active journal

c. The notary journal can be shared with other notaries

d. The notary journal is only required for specific acts of commission

Answer B

California law requires that all notaries keep an active journal; each notary act must be documented in the Journal. There are serious penalties for not keeping a journal, which also has to be stored in a safe and secure place.

29. If a notary public changes the business address to a different county, the local county clerk's office must be notified of a new oath of office and bond within what period of time?

a. Five business days

b. Ten business days

c. Fifteen business days

d. 30 business days

Answer D

When a notary has a physical change in address, he needs to file for a new oath of office and secure a bond. All this has to be done within 30 business days.

30. A retiring notary fails to deliver his Journal to the county clerk at the end of his commission. In the eyes of the law, he may be guilty of a:

a. Misdemeanor

b. Felony

c. Wilful neglect

d. Infarction

Answer A

Failure to deliver a journal to the county clerk at the end of your commission is deemed to be a misdemeanor.

Practice Test 5

1. When a notary makes a name change, the wilful failure to notify the Secretary of State or the local county clerk's office can result in a fine of?

a. $250

b. $500

c. $750

d. $1,000

Answer B

Willful failure can result when the Secretary of State is not notified of a name or address change; the penalty is $500

2. To become a commissioned notary in California, the applicant must?

a. Be fingerprinted

b. Pass a lie detector test

c. Have no more than one prior DUI conviction

d. Be an American citizen

Answer A

All candidates who pass the exam will be forwarded a form for fingerprints as part of the background check. Only candidates who pass will receive the fingerprint request. This is mandatory prior to becoming a notary in California.

3. After 35 years, a notary in San Diego decides to retire. What should he do with the notary seal?

a. Return it to the secretary of state

b. Return it to his employer

c. Destroy it

d. Keep it as a memento

Answer C

The notary seal is the property of the notary, and once the commission has expired for whatever reason, the notary seal must be destroyed. It cannot be given to anyone.

4. After a complaint was made against a new notary, a peace officer went to his office and requested the notary journal. The notary refused to provide the notary journal. The penalty in such scenarios is:

a. $500 fine

b. $1,000 fine

c. $2,500 fine

d. $5,000 fine

Answer C

When a peace officer requests the notary's Journal, he or she has to give it up. Failure to do so can result in a civil penalty of $2,500.

5. For those Notaries who fail to file the bond and oath on time, what is the fee to reapply?

a. $10

b. $20

c. $40

d. $50

Answer B

When notaries fail to file the oath and bond on time with the county clerk, the fee to reapply is $20.

6. If a client makes false statements to a notary in order to get improper notarization, this can result in a charge of:

a. Misdemeanor

b. Felony

c. Wilful neglect

d. Wilful misdemeanor

Answer B

Making false statements by the signer to obtain improper notarization can result in a charge of a felony.

7. A notary realizes that she did not properly check the ID of a client. What is the penalty for using a false identification during the notarization process?

a. $500 fine

b. $750 fine

c. $1,000 fine

d. $1,500 fine

Answer D

The civil penalty for using a false identification during notarization can result in a fine of $1,500.

8. When a notary states a known false fact as true, the penalty is:

a. $1,000

b. $2,500

c. $5,000

d. $10,000

Answer D

The penalty for stating a known false fact as true is associated with a monetary penalty of $10,000.

9. After her commission expired, a notary failed to deliver the documents to the local county clerk's office. This is most likely a:

a. Felony

b. Wilful neglect

c. Misdemeanor

d. Infarction

Answer C

Failing to deliver the notary documents to the local county clerk's office after the commission has expired can result in a misdemeanor.

10. Once a journal is stolen, the notary public must notify the secretary of state within what time frame?

a. Immediately

b. Within three business days

c. Within seven business days

d. Within the first 30 days

Answer A

When a notary journal is destroyed or stolen, the notary must notify the local county clerk's office immediately.

11. If the notary seal is stolen, the notary must notify the Secretary of State within what time frame?

a. Immediately

b. Within three business days

c. Within seven business days

d. Within the first 30 days

Answer A

If the notary seal is stolen, the notary must immediately notify the local county clerk's office.

12. The local county clerk has requested a notary to

submit a photocopy of the notary's journal. Within what time period should the notary submit the requested paperwork?

a. Within three business days

b. Within a week

c. Within 15 days

d. Immediately

Answer C

Once the county clerk has requested photocopies of the journal, the notary must provide them within 15 days. Even if there is going to be a delay, the notary must respond in writing.

13. The notary has been asked to surrender his journal to a peace officer. Within what timeframe should the secretary of state be notified of the surrender?

a. Within 24 hours

b. Within three business days

c. Within ten days

d. At anytime

Answer C

Once a notary has been asked to surrender his journal to a peace officer, the local county clerk's office should be notified within ten days.

14. A new notary decides to cut corners and has been charged with fraud with the intent to harm the client. This illegal endeavor can lead to a civil penalty of:

a. $250

b. $500

c. $1,000

d. $1,500

Answer D

When a notary commits an act of fraud, dishonesty, or deceit with an intent to harm, this can result in a civil penalty of up to $1,500.

15. A notary has been named as a grantee in a recent real estate transaction. Is he able to notarize the document?

a. No

b. Yes

c. It depends on the value of the real estate

d. Yes, as long as he documents it in the journal

Answer A

In a real property transaction, the notary is named grantor or grantee. In California, the notary is not supposed to sign anything when it comes to real estate- it is against the law.

16. In general, a notary seal will not include which of the following?

a. Name of the notary commission

b. County where oath and bond were filed

c. The expiration date of the commission

d. Date of birth of the notary

Answer D

The notary seal usually does not include the date of birth of the notary. Some of the features it will include are the sequential ID number, the expiration date of the commission, and the name of the notary.

17. In a recent advertisement, a notary falsely claimed he was also a lawyer. The penalty for making a false statement in a notary advertisement is as follows:

a. $500 fine

b. $1,000 fine

c. $1,500 fine

d. $5,000 fine

Answer C

When notaries falsely advertise their services, the penalties are harsh. For one, California law bars notaries from giving legal advice. For the first offense, the penalty is $1,500, but the Secretary of State is at liberty to add other penalties like suspension of the commission or revoking the commission.

18. If the notary fails to safeguard the seal and journal, the penalty may include the following:

a. Suspension of the commission

b. Revocation of the commission

c. Refusal to issue a commission

d. All of the above

Answer D

Failure to safeguard the notary seal can lead to harsh penalties, which usually include a monetary fine and /or suspension or revocation of the commission.

19. What fees is the notary supposed to charge for a deposition?

a. $15

b. $20

c. $25

d. $30

Answer D

The notary can charge up to a maximum of $30. Only lawyers can charge more for their services.

20. In California, before a notary can go into practice, he or she has to:

a. Purchase a surety bond

b. Undergo an interview with the secretary of state

c. Have a good credit score

d. Have a place to practice

Answer A

Before a notary can practice, he needs to purchase a surety bond of $15,000 and take an oath.

21. What are the dimensions of the rectangular seal?

a. 1' x 2 ½'

b. 1.½' x 2'

c. 2' x 2'

d. 1.5' x 2 ½'

Answer A

The dimensions for the rectangular seal are 1" x 2 1/2," and the circular seal cannot have a diameter of more than 2 inches.

22. A notary is moving his office from San Diego to Los Angeles. Within what timeframe should he notify the Secretary of State of the change in office address?

a. Within a week

b. Within 15 days

c. Within 30 days

d. Immediately

Answer C

In general, when the notary moves his or her office to another city or county, the local county clerk or the Secretary of State must be notified within 30 days.

23. Because the notary was in a hurry, he failed to

administer an oath. This error can lead to a civil penalty of:

a. $250

b. $500

c. $750

d. $1,000

Answer C

Failure to administer an oath can result in a civil penalty of $750.

24. The only notary in town decides to raise his fees by 200%. Under California law, charging clients high fees can lead to a civil penalty of:

a. $250

b. $500

c. $750

d. $1,000

Answer C

Charging fees above the cap set by the Secretary of state can result in a monetary penalty. Currently, overcharging clients for notarial acts can result in a $750 fine.

25. An elderly notary in Orange County has been charged with negligence by failing to discharge his notary responsibilities. He can face a civil penalty of:

a. $250

b. $500

c. $750

d. $1,000

Answer C

Negligence and Failing to properly conduct notarial duties can result in a monetary penalty of $1,000.

26. A colleague of the notary is asking him to notarize a document that is clearly false. When individuals encourage notaries to perform improper acts, this is considered a?

a. Misdemeanor

b. Felony

c. Wilful neglect

d. Infarction

Answer A

Notarizing false documents wilfully can result in a misdemeanor. It is associated with a monetary penalty of $1,500.

27. If the notary fails to obtain the satisfactory evidence needed to clearly establish the identity of a single credible witness, he or she can be guilty of?

a. Infarction

b. Wilful misdemeanor

c. Negligent Failure

d. Felony

Answer B

Failing to satisfactorily identify the credible witness can result in a charge of a misdemeanor.

28. If the notary fails to obtain the satisfactory evidence needed to clearly establish the identity of a single credible witness, he or she can face what type of penalty?

a. Loss of commission

b. Incarceration x 3 months

c. $10,000 fine

d. Remedial course in ethics

Answer C

Failing to properly identify a credible witness can result in a monetary penalty of $10,000.

29. The notary sign-in is a relatively complex process with many steps. However, which of the following is not part of the Notary's duty?

a. Ensure that the signer has the right photo ID

b. Write down the details in the journal

c. Ensure that the seal print is clear and visible

d. Check the document for grammar and typos

Answer D

The notary's main responsibilities relate to the signature. While he or she needs to briefly know the contents of the document, the notary is not responsible for checking typos and grammar.

30. Acting as a notary on real estate documents can result in what type of penalty?

a. Warning

b. Loss of commission

c. Any amount of monetary fine

d. Incarceration

Answer C

Notaries who act on real estate documents can face monetary fines of any amount, depending on the case and type of document. In general, notaries in California are now allowed to sign real estate documents.

Practice Test 6

1. Notaries who seek reappointments should retake the notary exam every:

a. Two years

b. Three years

c. Four years

d. Five years

Answer C

The notary commission in California expires every four years. Then one needs to repeat the whole process of getting re-commissioned.

2. During the process of notarization, if the notary fails to administer the oath, the penalty is:

a. Incarceration x 2 months

b. $250 fine

c. $500 fine

d. $750 Fine

Answer D

Failure to administer an Oath can result in a monetary penalty of $750 for each incident. And the Secretary of State may add other penalties like a revocation or suspension of the commission.

3. If an ordinary citizen falsely acts as a notary, what type of charges may result?

a. Felony

b. Misdemeanor

c. Wilful neglect

d. Ignorance of the law

Answer B

Falsely Acting as a Notary can result in a charge of a misdemeanor. Borrowing another person's seal and acting as a notary is illegal. That is why notaries are supposed to lock up the seal and store it in a locked container.

4. You're about to notarize a certificate, but when you ask for the ID, the individual produced an expired license. In order for the ID to be valid, the expiration should not be more than what period of time

a. 12 months

b. 24 months

c. 36 months

d. 60 months

Answer D

All IDs should be valid or issued within five years. California law does allow for the use of IDs that are expired, provided they were issued within the past five years.

5. A notary in California can only notarize?

a. A passport

b. A marriage certificate

c. A driving license

d. Power of attorney

Answer D

From the above, a notary can only notarize or certify a copy of a power of attorney. Passports, driver's licenses, and marriage certificates are not supposed to be notarized by notaries.

6. When notarizing a power of attorney, a thumbprint is required in California. The penalty for missing the thumbprint on the document is:

a. $500

b. $1,000

c. $1,500

d. $2,500

Answer D

Thumbprints are essential when notarizing certain documents like a power of attorney. Missing a thumbprint can result in a penalty of $2,500 per incident. There are instances when the state audits the journal, and when a thumbprint is missing, the fines are totaled and must be paid.

7. If the notary fails to notify the Secretary of State about a change of address, this violation is considered to be:

a. Infarction

b. Misdemeanor

c. Felony

d. Wilful neglect

Answer A

Failure to notify the Secretary of State about a change in address within 30 days is considered an infarction. Wilful failure to notify the Secretary can result in a fine of $500.

8. When a notary is charged with a disciplinary violation of his duties, in addition to disciplinary sanctions, the violation is punishable by a maximum civil penalty of:

a. $500

b. $750

c. $1,000

d. $1,500

Answer D

Violations of duties and responsibilities can result in a

wilful misdemeanor that is associated with a monetary penalty of $1,500.

9. When a notary public knowingly performs a notarial act with the intent of defrauding a deed or trust on real estate property, this is considered to be

a. Felony

b. Misdemeanor

c. Wilful neglect

d. Infarction

Answer A

When a notary wilfully and knowingly commits a notarial act with the intention of defrauding a deed on a property, this is considered to be a felony.

10. A 67-year-old notary public is removed from office. According to the law, all notarial documents should be

delivered to the county clerk's office within what period of time?

a. Seven business days

b. Fifteen business days

c. 30 business days

d. 60 business days

Answer C

If the notary is disqualified, resigns, or retires, then all the notarial documents must be delivered to the county clerk's office within 30 days.

11. If the surety of a notary wants to be released from the accountability of future acts, the release can be done by:

a. Verbal cancellation

b. Withdrawing services without a phone call

c. Making an application to the superior court in the local county

d. Placing an ad in the newspaper

Answer C

When a surety of a notary wants to be released from the responsibility on account of future notary acts, a written application to the superior court where the notary's business is located is required.

12. A notary public is disqualified from office and no longer eligible for reappointment. If the individual fails to deliver the notary documents to the local county clerk's office within 30 days, he/she is guilty of:

a. Infarction

b. Wilful neglect

c. Felony

d. Misdemeanor

Answer D

Once a notary is no longer active, retired, or disqualified, he or she must deliver all the notarial documents to the county clerk's office within 30 days. Failing to do so can result in a misdemeanor, plus be liable for any damages if the individual suffers from that inaction.

13. Once a notary public has delivered all the notary documents to the local county clerk's office, the records will be destroyed after what period of time?

a. Twelve months

b. Six months

c. Five years

d. Ten years

Answer D

In general, all records delivered to the county clerk's

office will be destroyed after ten years if there is no request made for the documents within this time.

Made in the USA
Las Vegas, NV
14 August 2023

76068393R00164